D1585477

Tantric Love:
Feeling Versus
Emotion

Golden Rules to
Make Love Easy

First published by O Books, 2010
O Books is an imprint of John Hunt Publishing Ltd., The Bothy, Deershot Lodge, Park Lane, Ropley,
Hants, SO24 0BE, UK
office1@o-books.net
www.o-books.net

Distribution in:	South Africa
	Stephan Phillips (pty) Ltd
UK and Europe	Email: orders@stephanphillips.com
Orca Book Services	Tel: 27 21 4489839 Telefax: 27 21 4479879
orders@orcabookservices.co.uk	
Tel: 01202 665432 Fax: 01202 666219	Text copyright Diana & Michael Richardson 2009
Int. code (44)	
	Design: Stuart Davies
USA and Canada	
NBN	ISBN: 978 1 84694 283 9
custserv@nbnbooks.com	
Tel: 1 800 462 6420 Fax: 1 800 338 4550	All rights reserved. Except for brief quotations
	in critical articles or reviews, no part of this
Australia and New Zealand	book may be reproduced in any manner without
Brumby Books	prior written permission from the publishers.
sales@brumbybooks.com.au	
Tel: 61 3 9761 5535 Fax: 61 3 9761 7095	The rights of Diana & Michael Richardson as
	author have been asserted in accordance with
Far East (offices in Singapore, Thailand,	the Copyright, Designs and Patents Act 1988.
Hong Kong, Taiwan)	
Pansing Distribution Pte Ltd	
kemal@pansing.com	A CIP catalogue record for this book is available
Tel: 65 6319 9939 Fax: 65 6462 5761	from the British Library.

Author photographs and Front cover photograph by Shobha, Sicilia

Printed by Digital Book Print

O Books operates a distinctive and ethical publishing philosophy in all areas of its business, from its global network of authors to production and worldwide distribution.

Tantric Love:
Feeling Versus Emotion

Golden Rules to
Make Love Easy

Diana & Michael Richardson

BOOKS

Winchester, UK
Washington, USA

CONTENTS

Contents

Dedicated to Osho's Vision for Humanity

"E é pra você
e pra todo mundo que quer trazer assim
a paz no coração"

"For you
and for everyone who wants to carry
peace in the heart"

Song "Gabriel" by Beto Guedes

Preface by Eva-Maria Zurhorst

Author of best selling *Love yourself... and it doesn't matter who you marry.*

If you are just browsing in a bookstore and open this book, and you have not yet read Diana Richardson, you may be asking yourself "Is *'Tantric Love: Feeling versus Emotion'* the right book for me?" Then I can tell you that for me the books written by Diana Richardson (and now for the first time with her partner) are the most important books that I read over the past years.

After recommending, as a therapist and couples consultant, her previous books, *The Heart of Tantric Sex* and *Tantric Orgasm for Women*, to many people, I am delighted to find more material with *Tantric Love: Feeling versus Emotion*. I am also glad to find an opportunity here to express my enthusiasm and gratefulness for the approach which I discovered through the books of Diana Richardson. I felt a deep relief for finally I found an answer beyond positions, techniques, fantasies and the endless search for the perfect lover. I also found a new path, which is explained in her books in a way that is both concrete and practicable.

This new book is dedicated to a theme that dominates and steers our lives – emotions. Emotions obstruct our outlook on love, and impede the very thing that we most long for: to be present and fulfilled, and able to enter into a deep connection with others. What is the difference between emotions and feelings? How can you learn to free yourself from these unconscious forces? You can discover this directly from this book! As Diana Richardson writes, 'We live in order to love – nothing is truer than that. We are here because of love and it is love that keeps us alive.'

Eva-Maria Zurhorst, Germany, 2006.

Acknowledgements

We extend our gratitude and appreciation to the couples who have permitted us to publish their personal experiences in distinguishing between feeling and emotion. Thank you to Miguel Ruiz and Eckhart Tolle for their kind permission to use excerpts from their writings. We are eternally grateful for the presence of Osho, our spiritual master, and our thanks are due to Osho Foundation International for permitting the use of Osho's inspiring words.

Authors' Note

Diana & Michael Richardson

The books *The Heart of Tantric Sex, Tantric Orgasm for Women* and *Tantric Sex for Men* include a chapter on the significant theme of emotions. In *Tantric Love: Feeling versus Emotion*, the material on emotions has been lifted out of the sexual context and amplified. Now it appears as a separate and self contained book because the information on 'feelings and emotions' is of equal significance, whether a person is interested in exploring sex (and therefore more likely to read our books) or not. However, as sex and emotions are frequently linked, there will be several necessary references to sex. There is no direct sexual guidance as in our other books.

An insight into 'emotionality' is valid for each and every individual, whether they are single or in a partnership. We have now been working with couples for over twenty years, during which time we have observed that the information that we present on how to differentiate between 'feelings and emotions' during our week long 'Making Love' Retreats, has a profound and positive impact. It enables couples to sustain love, instead of experiencing love as something unstable, with highs and lows.

Most of the unhappiness on earth is a by-product of emotion. If we are to witness a shift toward light and love on earth, for which we pray, a new awareness of emotion and its destructive consequences will have to be central to this change. Emotion operates 'unconsciously' in us and there is an urgent need to notice when it is 'active'. Many people today feel helpless and powerless against the forces of unconsciousness present in our society. Even so, we must not lose heart or give up personal responsibility. As individuals we really are in a position to contribute lovingly toward peace through questioning unconscious negative emotional patterns, which lie at the root of most of our unhappiness.

Living is for loving, nothing else really rings clear and true. Love is why we are here, the light that encourages us to keep moving forward. When we have the capacity to recognize our 'emotional side', and with constructive 'golden rules' to hand, we empower ourselves to live joyfully, where love can be sustained as a subtle, yet vibrant, ever present current flowing through life.

Books by the same Authors:

Diana Richardson
The Heart of Tantric Sex
A Unique guide to Love and Sexual fulfillment
O Books, 2002 (first published 1999 as *The Love Keys*)

Diana Richardson
Tantric Orgasm for Women
Destiny Books, 2004

Diana Richardson & Michael Richardson
Tantric Sex for Men
Making Love a Meditation
Destiny Books, 2010

Diana Richardson
Tantric Love Letters
Questions and Answers
O Books, due 2011

Chapter 1

LOVE IS NOT AN EMOTION

Ups and Downs of Love

Perhaps you have noticed that so often, when you ask a friend about their love life, you receive a standard reply. And it does not seem to matter which friend you are talking to. Perhaps you realize that you too say the same words yourself. The well worn phrase is 'up and down, you know how it goes'.

These few words are repeated again and again, and through repetition the phrase has by now become a hypnotic mantra which we all unwittingly associate with love – love is unstable. A change of partners does not seem to make a difference to the situation either. As soon as the honeymoon is over the talk about love's 'ups and downs' begins.

Interestingly, when you listen more closely to others or yourself, the mantra actually begins as a statement, 'up and down' but in fact it ends as a question, 'you know how it goes?' Usually there will be a slight rise in voice intonation accompanying the words, 'you know how it goes?' The inflection in the voice communicates to the listener that a question is being asked to the effect 'you have the same don't you?' or 'your experience is similar, isn't it?' The implied 'question' creates a feeling of fellowship, a sense of mutual bonding. The other person is automatically included in the statement/question, because their experience of love will also usually consist of 'ups and downs'.

Belief that Love is Out of Our Hands

It is incredible to realize that we all live under the impression that love is a phenomenon which fluctuates, and that we are powerless against it. We are all hypnotizing ourselves by thinking, saying, and believing love to be unreliable and unsteady. Through this hypnosis we unconsciously create unhappy situations for ourselves. We experience love as an accidental force and believe there is nothing we can consciously do to keep love alive. These beliefs reflect that we know very little about love, because the truth of love is quite different to our experience of it.

What is Love?

Love is overflowing joy. Love is when you have seen who you are; then there is nothing left except to share your being with others. Love is when you have seen that you are not separate from existence. Love is when you have felt an organic, orgasmic unity with all that is. Love is not a relationship. Love is a state of being; it has nothing to do with anybody else. One is not in love, one is love. And of course when one is love, one is in love – but that is an outcome, a by-product, that is not the source. The source is that one is love.

Osho, transcribed teachings, The Guest, *Vol. 6*

Remember, love is born with you; it is your intrinsic quality. All that is needed is to give it way – to make a passage for it, to let it flow, to allow it to happen. We are all blocking it, holding it back. We are so miserly about love, for the simple reason that we have been taught a certain economics. That economics is perfectly right about the outside world: if you have so much money and you go on giving that money to people, soon you will be a beggar, soon you will have to beg yourself. By giving money you will lose it. This economics, this arithmetic has entered into our blood, bones and marrow. It is true about the outside world – nothing is wrong in it – but it is not true about the inner journey. There, a totally different arithmetic functions: the more you give, the more you have; the less you give, the less you have. If you don't give at all you will lose your natural qualities. They will become stagnant, closed; they will go under-

ground. Finding no expression they will shrink and die.

Osho, transcribed teachings, Come, Come, Yet again come, *Vol. 10*

Turn Inward to Find Love

To begin to shift our perspective and *personal experience of love* we have to realize that love *is*; love is not something that goes up and down. The enlightened masters tell us that 'love is a state of being, an organic, orgasmic unity with all that is'. Day by day we are surrounded by the awesome miracle of creation, a manifestation and expression of pure love. Love actually *is* all around us!

Be silent as you sit somewhere, close your eyes, and fall back into your heart, and remember the moments when you did feel 'in love', even if briefly. As you shift your attention from outside to inside, and relax into your body, you will always find love alive vibrating delicately and gently in your heart. Love is a 'state', an intrinsic quality that resides within the being; how can there possibly be highs and lows? There may be moments when we are not in contact with our love, but this does not mean that love has up and left us for good.

Emotion Goes Up and Down

Once we realize that love is an ever-present happening in the core of our system, the next question is to ask 'what actually *is* going up and down?' What is taking place when we feel ourselves suddenly 'fall out of love', out of connection with ourselves and another person? What is happening when suddenly the world turns upside down and we find ourselves blaming someone, making them responsible for our unhappiness? What happens when unexpectedly the tide turns and the loving flow between us is disturbed and interrupted for hours or days?

How often has it happened to you, that within a fraction of a second, the person you love the most in this world turns into the one you like the least? You will discover, or at least get a hint of what goes up and down when you begin to examine anew the very moment you 'fall out of love' with your partner.

Love is not an Emotion

At the moment of disconnection what you are experiencing is a *rise* in your level of emotions. And you will have noticed how that surge or wave of emotion instantly and utterly obscures all loving feelings and loving vibrations.

> *Love is not to be a part of your emotions. Ordinarily that's what people think and experience, but anything overwhelming is very unstable. It comes like a wind and passes by, leaving you behind, empty, shattered, in sadness and in sorrow.*
>
> *According to those who know man's whole being – his mind, his heart and his being – love has to be an expression of your being, not an emotion. Emotion is very fragile, very changing. One moment it seems that is all. Another moment you are simply empty. So the first thing to do is to take love out of this crowd of overwhelming emotions. Love is not overwhelming. On the contrary, love is a tremendous insight, clarity, sensitivity, awareness. But that kind of love rarely exists, because very few people ever reach to their being.*
>
> Osho, transcribed teachings, Om Shanti, Shanti, Shanti, 17

Chapter 2

EMOTIONS ARE DIFFERENT
TO FEELINGS

Now with the understanding that love is not to be a part of our emotions, we can begin to make a separation between our warm inner heart-filled feelings and our emotions. In general, as we speak about ourselves or situations, we use the words 'emotions' and 'feelings' interchangeably, as if the experience of 'emotion' is almost the same as the experience of 'feeling'. But emotions are definitely *not* the same as feelings. As you explore your inner world you will soon observe that emotions and feelings are different. In reality they are two diametrically opposite experiences. The experience of a feeling is a world apart from the experience of an emotion.

Emotion Past and Feeling Present

The vital difference between emotion and feeling is that emotions have their roots in the *past*, and feelings relate to the *present* moment. *Emotions represent our feelings which were not previously expressed, and these accumulate with time.*

During our week-long Making Love seminars we introduce the theme of emotion only on the fourth day. We explain and apologize to the couples that we are unable to talk about emotions any earlier, even though we know emotions are responsible for major disturbances in most relationships. The reason for our delay in giving the material on emotions is because the initial days are devoted to teaching couples how to tune into the source of love lying within each person: to be present and experience love as the 'radiance of their being'. With a completely fresh experience of love they are easily able to see emotion for the destructive force it is and realize that the unconsciousness of their emotions has caused a great deal of heartbreak and unhappiness in the past.

Indicators of Emotion

We ask our participants 'How does an emotional experience *feel*?' What do we experience in ourselves, in our bodies, when we are in emotion? The answers given in response to our questions are similar in each and every seminar.

Below is a list which describes the experience when suddenly the level of emotion rises and love equally as suddenly evaporates. Emotion is easily and immediately recognizable in the following experiences:

1. The sensation of *separation* or disconnection from the other person, as if a wall comes down between you, or you feel paralyzed.
2. It is difficult to meet the eyes of the other person, you *avoid eye contact*, or they appear to be far away in the distance.
3. You *blame* the other person for the situation or for your unhappiness.
4. You use the words 'you *never*... do such and such' or 'you *always*... do such and such'; you talk about the other person not yourself.
5. You become withdrawn and closed.
6. Your body is contracted, paralyzed, numb, sometimes with pains.
7. Your vision becomes narrow and cloudy.
8. You are exhausted, low in energy and wish to sleep.
9. You are protective and defensive.
10. You experience abandonment and rejection.
11. You experience loneliness and a sense of being incomplete.
12. You are self-righteous, with the attitude that 'I am right' and you refuse to give up until the other person *admits you are right*.

13. You experience yourself as being misunderstood or taken for granted.
14. You like to argue, discuss, fight and challenge the other.
15. Your mind is very active, full of negative thoughts and doubts.
16. The themes occur in repeating patterns, same issue again and again.
17. You experience helplessness and you are a victim of your situation.
18. Your outlook on life is hopeless and depressing.
19. You get tense and prickly (like a hedgehog) and the other person cannot do or say anything right.
20. The emotional state of separation/disconnection continues for hours or days before a return to harmony.
21. You try to change the other person.
22. You want to get revenge by saying or doing unkind, unloving things to them.
23. You react from ego, pride.
24. It is an unconscious pattern – you don't realize why you are reacting in that way.
25. The reaction relates to some incident/experience lying in the past.

The uncomfortable experiences listed above can be called the 'symptoms of emotion'. Usually you will suffer many symptoms simultaneously, and you may even observe other symptoms to add to the list! From now on, when one or some of these symptoms are present in you, you will begin to have the insight that you are *in emotion*; that something from the past has come into play here and now and taken over the show. In a way you were taken hostage by the emotions temporarily. It is helpful to remind yourself repeatedly that when you are emotional, the situation has little to do with the present. The emotion is resurfacing in the present of course, but you feel disconnected from the present. There has been a dramatic shift in your perception as a by-product of the accumulated and unresolved past which we all carry around with us, to a lesser or greater degree.

Easier to Recognize Emotion of the Other

Perhaps while reading the symptoms of emotion listed above you have already started to recognize a part of yourself. When we ask participants if they see themselves in the list there is an uproar in the room – yes, absolutely! Or perhaps you might have said to yourself, 'I, for sure, can see my partner!' as one man replied during a seminar once and his comment was greeted with a roar of knowing laughter by all!

Take note, it is easier to see the emotion of another than to see your own! The truth is that each of us intimately knows our own emotional side, and we experience the emotional side of other people too. However, we do not understand *how* our emotional side, which pops up from time to time, creates shadows of darkness or unhappiness in our lives. We have no inkling of how to view or deal with this 'shadow aspect' of ourselves. The under-standing of emotion, and its root in the past, is the missing piece in our self awareness. When we begin to acknowledge that there is an 'emotional' side to the human, we open a new door, and thereby create the potential to rise above the vortex of emotions which so easily obscure and damage our love.

Experience of Feelings

The experience of a 'feeling' and the experience of 'emotion' are really like day and night. Feelings, when they are expressed as they arise *in the present*, lead to to a completely different inner experience. We ask couples how they feel in themselves when they share from the heart, expressing their deeper feelings. Interestingly, the feedback we receive about feelings *contradicts* the previous list of the emotional indicators. Words given to describe the experience of expressing a feeling are almost the *opposite* of the words given to describe the experience of emotion. The two experiences are definitely not the same.

We ask 'When you truly express how you feel, when you share your deepest feelings, do you experience separation between you and your partner?'

'No, of course not, we feel wonderfully connected.'

'Can you look your partner in the eye?'

'Yes! Easy.'

'Are you contracted and collapsed?'

'No, expanded and alive.'

'Is your attitude closed, protective and defensive?'

'No, open, soft and vulnerable.'

And so on we continue down the list of emotions asking for the corresponding words to describe how they feel *when they are able to express what they feel in the present.* Responses from our participants appear below. Each emotion is listed as in the previous section, and now after each symptom of the emotional experience appears the opposite feeling experience.

List of Emotions Versus Feelings

When you have expressed your deeper feelings:

1. Instead of separation and disconnection from the other person – *you feel connected and closer.*
2. Before it was difficult to meet the eyes of the person – *now eye contact is easy.*
3. Instead of blaming the other person – *you are acknowledging yourself and expressing your deeper feelings.*
4. You do not say 'you never' or 'you always' and talk about the other – *you say 'I feel...' and talk about yourself.*
5. You are not withdrawn and closed – *you are open and receptive.*
6. Instead of the body getting collapsed, contracted, paralyzed – *the body opens, you feel expanded, alive.*

7. Your narrow, negative, cloudy outlook - *becomes wide, clear vision with a positive outlook.*

8. Instead of being exhausted – *you are inwardly refreshed.*

9. Instead of being protective, defensive – *you feel vulnerable, open, innocent.*

10. Instead of abandonment and rejection – *you feel embraced, accepted.*

11. Instead of loneliness and a sense of being incomplete – *you feel complete, all-one (alone).*

12. You are not self-righteous – *you are self revealing.*

13. You are not misunderstood or taken for granted – *you feel understood and appreciated.*

14. Instead of wanting to argue and discuss – *you want to exchange, share.*

15. Instead of being in the mind, thought oriented, full of doubt – *you are connected to your body and heart, in trust.*

16. Instead of repeating patterns – *things become spontaneous, changing.*

17. Instead of being a victim, helpless – *you feel empowered.*

18. Instead of hopelessness – *you are full of trust.*

19. You feel tense – *you can relax.*

20. It lasts for days – *you move on quickly.*

21. You try to change the other person – *you accept them as they are.*

22. Instead of getting revenge – *you feel loving.*

23. Instead of reacting with ego and pride – *you respond with heart and love.*

24. Instead of operating unconsciously – *you are being conscious.*

25. You are relating to the past – *a happening in the present.*

Feelings Only Talk about Self not Other

Essential to expression of feelings one is naturally talking only about oneself, and *not* the other person. Any sentence would start with 'I feel...'. Definitely not 'I feel that *you*......'! Which is a way of indirectly blaming the other person, and is a sure sign of leaking your own emotions and not taking responsibility for them.

The usual resolution to the emotional stalemate reached in domestic arguments is that one partner will finally break down into expressing their underlying feelings, their vulnerability, insecurity, and pain. We have all had the experience how reconnection and togetherness is instantly created when one person gives up the fight, when the ego melts away from the heart and the tears begin to flow.

The return to innocence, connecting to the true feeling, has an alchemical effect on the situation, and the other person naturally lays down their weapons and opens up their hearts and arms again. As soon as the ego, which temporarily obscures the heart, is put to the side, love will surface again. Love does not disappear in these moments of emotion, as couples so often experience, it lies shining behind the ego gently waiting, radiant and ever-present.

Feelings Contacted Through Heart and Body

Relax into the body and heart to experience yourself and 'feel' deep inside to discover the subtle sensations and sensitivities within. Find words to express the subtle. Avoid general words like 'it feels good'. Instead, be more accurate; the word 'good' could mean warm, inspired, happy, excited, relieved or a whole other range of experiences. When we are general about what we feel then words such as good and nice *prevent the other person from connecting easily* with what we might actually be experiencing within ourselves. Fall into your heart and your body to discover your true inner feelings. Express and share your feelings as they arise, and as they change.

Marshall Rosenberg, in his book called *Nonviolent Communication - a language of life* (page 44/45), which comes highly recommended, has compiled an A-Z list of words to help increase the power to articulate feelings, and to be able to clearly describe a whole range of experiences. For example, instead of saying you feel 'fine' you could instead expand on yourself and say you feel absorbed, adventurous, affectionate, alert, alive, amazed, amused, animated, appreciative, ardent, aroused, astonished, satisfied, secure, sensitive, serene, spellbound, splendid, stimulated, surprised, tender, thankful, thrilled, touched, tranquil, trusting...

Osho suggests that one can also make a practice of encouraging pure feelings such as friendliness, compassion, cheerfulness and gratefulness. These four feelings each have their opposite. The opposite of friendliness is hatred and enmity. The opposite of compassion is cruelty, violence and unkindness. The opposite of cheerfulness is sadness, misery, anguish and worry. The opposite of gratitude is ingratitude. Someone whose life and emotions are in the four opposite aspects is in a state of impure emotions. And someone who is rooted in the first four aspects is rooted in pure feelings. When we consciously practice being friendly, cheerful, grateful and compassionate we begin to refine ourselves and tune into the higher vibration of love.

In most people's lives our pure feelings have moved into the opposite negative emotional expression. By encouraging positive feelings you can change the quality of your day. Be grateful for all that life has showered on you. For the small simple gifts that come with each day. Do not compare yourself with other people, it is a futile exercise. Start to see your cup as half full and not as half empty. When we begin to feel gratitude we feel full, positive and affirmed, not empty, cheated and miserable.

Osho, transcribed teachings. The path of Meditation

Love is Ever-Present in the Body

Love will have many bodily feelings associated with it which we do not normally identify as love. When we take the awareness into the body, and tune into ourselves on a cellular level, any place we feel vibrant, alive, warm, tingling, is a place where love is *already* alive and well. You can feel love vibrating cellularly within you. Perhaps a glowing, an expansion, spaciousness, gratitude, a total 'yes' to life, a deep sense of well-being. Love is a 'state of being' deeply rooted in the body, arising in the core and radiating outward. In love, another person enhances or reflects your very own inner beauty. Again and again relax inwardly into your body to maintain a connection to the beauty and delight of your inner aliveness. By holding the inner sensations of love in the bodily awareness they are encouraged and enhanced.

Fear to Love

Many of us are 'afraid' to open ourselves up to love because of the imprints our previous experiences have left on us. We have been hurt through love, we have had our love rejected, all kinds of 'agony' happen in the name of love. Reacting out of self preservation and fear we avoid getting too close to people, showing our vulnerability, and allowing intimacy to grow between us. Fear tends to dominate us and we become unadventurous in love.

Question addressed to Osho:

You say fear is the opposite of love. Have you any practical or impractical suggestions how one can drop fear?

Response: *Love is existential; fear is only the absence of love. And the problem with any absence is that you cannot do anything directly about it.*

Fear is like darkness. What can you do about darkness directly? You cannot drop it, you cannot throw it out, you cannot bring it in. There is no way to relate with darkness without bringing light in. The way to darkness goes via light. If you want darkness, put the light off; if you don't want darkness, put the light on. But you will have to do something with light, not with darkness at all.

The same is true about love and fear: love is light, fear is darkness. The person who becomes obsessed with fear will never be able to resolve the problem. It is like wrestling with darkness – you are bound to be exhausted sooner or later, tired and defeated. And the miracle is, defeated by something which is not there at all! And when one is defeated, one certainly feels how powerful the darkness is, how powerful is fear, how powerful is ignorance, how powerful is the unconscious. And they are not powerful at all – they don't exist in the first place.

Never fight with the non-existential. That's where all the ancient religions got lost. Once you start fighting with the non-existential you are doomed. Your small river of consciousness will be lost in the non-existential desert – and it is infinite.

Osho, transcribed teachings, Come, Come, Yet again Come, 10

Fear is just the opposite of love. Remember, hate is not the opposite of love, as people think; hate is love standing upside down, it is not the opposite of love. The real opposite of love is fear. In love one expands, in fear one shrinks. In fear one becomes closed, in love one opens. In fear one doubts, in love one trusts. In fear one is left lonely, in love one disappears; hence there is no question of loneliness at all. When one is not, how can one be lonely?

Osho, transcribed teachings, The Guest 6

Fear is Opposite of Love

We can say that in general 'emotions' fall under the umbrella of 'fear', while 'feelings' fall under the umbrella of 'love.' If we observe ourselves when we are in emotion, we can usually describe ourselves generally to be in a state of fear, and doubt; we shrink and contract. And the state of fear represents the absence of love. When we are in 'love', when all our needs are being met, we feel expanded, open, trusting.

Start Loving!

The first thing to remember is: don't make a problem out of fear. Love is the question. Something can be done about love immediately; there is no need to wait or postpone. Start loving! And it is a natural gift from God to you, or from the whole, whichever term you like. If you are brought up in a religious way, then God; if you are not brought up in a religious way, then the whole, the universe, the existence.

Osho, transcribed teachings, Come, come, yet again come #10

Chapter 3

EMOTION IS TOXIC

Awareness of Triggers

You have noticed perhaps that when a person is in an emotional state it is usually quite visible. They lose their inner light and shine, and become dark, withdrawn or stormy. When there is a shift into an emotionally distorted reality it will happen very fast as if a switch has been flipped. In an instant our past becomes active and starts reverberating inside us. In casual conversation many of us will use the words 'he/she pushed my buttons'. This phrase means that another person's words or actions caused a disturbance in you and triggered an uncomfortable reaction. The interesting fact is that we seem to know that our 'buttons' exist. We also seem to know that they are active, alive and well, and sensitive to certain types of pressure. So what is stirred up inside us when we become emotional? What exactly is this dark force that pushes its way through the body and envelops us? What makes us feel so bad and unhappy? What lies at the root of the emotion? We know the symptoms, what is the cause?

As already briefly mentioned in the previous chapter, our emotion represents all the unexpressed feelings stored up inside us. Emotion is the outcome of *not* expressing feelings in the past when the feeling was actually happening; not saying *what* you felt *when* you felt it. Emotion is the by-product of repressing feelings, pushing everything down, bottling them up inside. Our inner unresolved feelings begin to resonate when there is a suitable outer trigger. As soon as the button is pushed the unlived feelings become active inside us again, just like a tape recorder with a replay button.

Emotions are Toxic

Another indicator of emotion is that the overwhelming reaction a person experiences is usually *disproportional to the trigger*. A slight provocation can cause a huge eruption of emotion. This indicates that unexpressed feelings stored within us are under some pressure, and the emotion finds ways to vent itself and so relieve the inner pressure and tension. Unexpressed feelings turn sour in the system, which explains why when we are 'in emotion' we like to take revenge and hurt the other person, trying desperately to get back at them. When we do not express our feelings in the present, the tension stays inside and slowly festers like a wound and in time it becomes poisonous and as a result we suffer and someone else suffers too.

Emotions, our toxins from unexpressed feelings, are determined to be discharged or released sooner or later. Sadly it is frequently the person or people closest to us that we regularly deposit our poison on! The toxins that are part and parcel of emotion can in time gradually destroy love. Ongoing bouts of emotion in a relationship can be visualized as a slow process of soil erosion. When there is a flood of water down a hill some soil gets washed away. Each flood and the hillside is eaten up a little more. Before you know it the landscape is full of deep valleys and ravines that appear impossible to bridge. In the same way, each time we fight, emotion eats up a piece of precious love, the next time a bit more. Eventually we look at the person we supposedly 'fell in love' with and begin to ask 'What happened to our love?'

Many couples have told us that they separated from a previous partner because they had *one fight too many*. They finally could not track their way back to love, as they had done on previous occasions, and as a result, the relationship was over. The danger of frequent emotional attacks in a relationship is that emotions can and will extinguish all loving feelings between two people in time. Love is like a delicate and fragile flower which cannot always survive the toxicity of emotional fights and arguments. Love more easily reveals itself in an atmosphere of tranquility and contentment than in a haphazard war zone.

Unconscious Leaking of Emotion

Emotion is commonly leaked unconsciously in nagging, chronic complaining about all sorts of things, arguing about meaningless details, contradicting as a matter of habit, being defensive, brittle and irritable. When we are emotional it is not easy for others to do the right thing by us, everything they say or do is wrong. If we do not find fault with our partner but get impatient with the cashier in the supermarket and ruin her day, we are being emotional! If we get angry while driving the car or we get repeatedly exasperated with the children, we are being emotional.

If you have these kind of experiences often it is helpful to realize that you are in all likelihood somewhat emotional and now is perhaps the time to do something about it. Avoid spreading unhappiness as you move through life. If you spread unhappiness you will receive unhappiness in return. If you give love and spread love around you, you will receive love in return and in abundance.

Low Grade Emotionality

Some men and women have come up to us during our seminars, and told us that they do not experience the shift that we describe, from connection to separation, from expansion to contraction, from feeling to emotion. In fact, they tell us that a more accurate way to describe their daily experience is one of *subtle disconnection all the time*. Not greatly disconnected, but on a low level there exists an experience of separation and loneliness. You have the blues, find yourself in a mildly depressed state.

Such an experience of ongoing subtle separation can be described as one of 'low-grade' emotionality. When emotion is low grade it resembles a very slight fever, which is not acute and does not produce a real temperature, but affects the health of the system on delicate levels nonetheless. If you recognize you are in a state of low grade emotionality where the psyche and whole view of life is negatively influenced, we suggest that you begin to move your body on a regular basis as explained in the steps suggested in chapter 7 on how to actually deal with emotion when you are emotional. These so called 'golden rules' apply to both high-grade (acute) and low-grade (chronic) emotion, and give *constructive keys to dissolving* undercurrents of unhappiness and discontent infiltrating our lives.

Low grade emotionality also manifests in silently brooding in a withdrawn way or thinking repeatedly how the other person is wrong in everything they do or say. You find yourself blaming them, internally resenting them and creating separation for yourself.

In moments of emotionality it is advised that you drink a large glass of pure water because water will help to dilute the toxins present in the system. After a drink there can be a noticeable shift within, as if the edge has been taken off the intensity of what you are experiencing. Naturally, water in itself is unlikely to solve the whole problem but it represents a step in the right direction. Taking a shower when you are emotional, or after a bout of emotion, will help to wash away your toxic negativity and leave you feeling refreshed and more present.

Personal sharing from a man:

I recognized much about emotion and feeling in your teachings. It is not so easy to practice it in the very moment – mostly I notice later, but that is better than to stay in the emotion and have no way out. Here is what happened to me during the workshop: My wife and I were in your workshop. While making love we expressed our feelings. Then she said one sentence; it was something she said many times before... I felt hopeless; now we are here to take a new step and something like this is happening... I felt self-pity, like a victim and there was a big distance between us. After a while of searching for a reason, I was suddenly aware about the situation – I am caught in my emotions!

The next moment I became aware that understanding and explaining is not going to be of any help to me here now. Instead, I kept my focus on my body and my breathing. In the past I would have become more and more confused. Suddenly, realizing what was happening inside me, it felt like the sky was clearing and the sun shining again. I could look into her eyes and was able to feel my love for her again. We are beginning to differentiate between emotions and feelings in our daily life, sometimes difficult and sometimes good, but we are definitely on our way.

Chapter 4

BE AWARE OF EMOTION

Individual Commitment

If it is your wish to grow in love and consciousness as an individual and attract more love and joy it becomes necessary to develop an awareness of your emotions. Begin to notice your 'emotionality', how the level of your emotion rises and falls through the days and weeks. To free oneself of emotionality is to begin shedding a clinging layer of unhappiness, hardness and negativity that stifles our life force and prevents us from feeling the joy of our innate beauty and love.

Transforming emotion does not depend on another person, it is something each individual can and must do for him- or herself. Naturally other people will be involved in the process but they are incidental because the commitment is personal and individual. To take responsibility for emotions is the way to invite light and love into each day of your life.

Awareness as a Transformational Tool

Any self enquiry automatically requires the awareness, the observer, the witness, the ability to watch the show from the outside while being centre stage at the same time. Awareness is basic to self transformation and we can develop 'awareness' on three different levels – of the body, of the mind and of the emotions. Emotion, of the three, is the most subtle level and not so easy to detect.

Awareness on Body Level

To develop awareness on a body level is relatively easy; we can feel it from the inside as a world in itself, an endless source of delicate delightful sensation. From the outside we can stroke and touch the body to amplify our awareness. Or we can keep awareness in both feet while walking for example, feeling intensified contact to the ground, the pleasurable pressure and weight shifts with each step. The body is a natural bridge to the present moment where life is happening in the here and now. Awareness within your body increases the love and respect for it as truly a temple of love, joy and bliss.

Love is literally to be felt in the body as mentioned in chapter 2, *so remember to feel the love that you are.* Use your body as a bridge and begin to view it as a best friend that exists forever in the now. Focusing directly on the physical body helps us to step down from mind's nagging negative thoughts entangled in the past or in the future. *The body is an ongoing here and now experience, and holding the body in the awareness keeps us rooted in the now. The body exists only in the now, not in the future. The body knows today, not tomorrow.*

Using the body as a bridge to the present requires an inward orientation basic to the teachings of Tantra. Personally, we express it as the shift from 'up and out' or extrovert as we are conditioned to be, to one of living 'in and down' in our bodies, more 'introverted or inverted', and connected to the inner, the being, the source of love lying within.

Awareness on Mind Level

To develop an awareness of the mind and its endless chattering is not as easy as focusing on the body. As an unconscious habit most people easily drift off into thinking, day dreaming about the future, or lingering over memories from the past. And we can get *so* involved in reminiscing that a long period of time passes without *actually* noticing that we are totally absent to the present, lost in thinking.

Mind prevents us from being fully present in our bodies and to our reality. We disconnect again and again from the 'now', and have little or no reference to our bodies or awareness of ourselves in these moments. During mind-absorbed obsessive thinking we stop feeling ourselves and can easily completely forget that we even posses such a thing as this physical body. Noticing you are caught up in thinking is a more elusive process than being aware of body. Our tendency is to identify more with mind and thinking, past and future than with the present and body sensations. We tend to treat the body like a machine and use it in a mechanical, uncaring, unconscious way. This attitude has reduced the sensitivity of our bodies and which in turn also contributes to an emphasis on the mind, thinking, daydreaming, and reminiscing. The body has basically moved out of our general awareness and there is not much to be felt or experienced on an inner cellular level.

Awareness on Emotion Level

As already mentioned, of the three levels, emotion is the most subtle and slippery layer to pinpoint with the awareness. The difficulty lies in the *identification* with our emotional side. When we are *in* emotion we believe that we *are* the emotion – that *this is totally me* or I am this! Emotion is such an overwhelming and all consuming experience we have the belief that emotion is an intrinsic part and expression of ourselves – it truly is *who* we are.

The closeness of the emotional experience, the identification with the intensity of emotion occurs because when emotion is activated it is felt strongly on a physical plane. The toxic emotion uses our body temporarily. This physical experience gives us the distinct impression that emotion is *who* we are. Some people delight in proudly claiming that they are very emotional, as they perceive 'emotion' as a positive quality. They view their ranting and ravings as an authentic expression of themselves, whereas in reality often they are in contact with accumulated unexpressed feelings from the past that are not really associated with the present.

27

Emotion is Felt in Connective Tissue

On a physical level, emotion, when it is activated, can be felt as a swirling sensation spiraling through the numerous layers of connective tissue (fascia) in the body. Fascia has the remarkable function of binding the body together to form one integrated whole. Circuits of fascia weave through the body circling from top to toe about five times, connecting and binding the deepest layers with the most superficial layers.

If you are alert, next time you get emotional observe your body and feel what is happening inside of you. In the very first few seconds you are likely to detect some kind of substance with density whirling or spiraling through your body. The sensations are due to the previously mentioned toxicity of emotion that enters the system. The toxins, all the poison stored in repressed feelings, are responsible for the dramatic shift in reality from heaven to hell.

Emotions and Solar Plexus

During your life in general become aware of your solar plexus. In particular, if you observe your body when you are emotional, you may become aware of a contraction, tension or pain in the solar plexus. For many the solar plexus and stomach area is an ongoing source of discomfort. The solar plexus is formed by a huge network of nerves and is a significant energy centre. If you push gently with your fingertips into the area between your navel and the tip of the breastbone (the area of the diaphragm) you will be touching the solar plexus area.

Our emotions, our unexpressed feelings, can cause tensions in the solar plexus. Perhaps you have noticed an immediate 'knot' in the solar plexus when someone makes a remark that 'gets to you', provokes you, and triggers your emotions. When we ask couples during our seminars if anyone feels discomfort in the solar plexus or upper stomach area, and good half of the people present will raise their hands, to confirm that they are aware of ongoing tension held in there. When a person gets emotional sometimes the smell of the breath can become putrid for the period they are emotional which shows the stomach and solar plexus area is definitely disturbed by the emotions.

Solar plexus can be a useful *monitor* for your emotions. Maintain awareness in the solar plexus during your daily activities and use it as an indicator to inform you of what is going on in your life. Sometimes you may not feel emotional as such, in separation and so on, but you may feel uncomfortable sensations in the solar plexus which are having a disturbing effect on your immediate reality. In such cases it is really useful to begin to go through your interactions of the day, consecutively, and attempt to identify precisely when the strange sensations began. At what moment did things change? When did you suddenly experience a disturbance in the solar plexus? What did someone say or do that made you react on an emotional level?

The simple step of identifying *when* the disturbance entered your system can help you dissolve some of the inner discomfort the emotion provoked. Pinning down the moment the disturbance was set in motion is helpful because then you *know* precisely what trigger from the outside had an impact on you. If you do not isolate the event and take responsibility, then there is the possibility that you continue for the rest of the day feeling ill at ease, a bit negative and complaining, without really realizing exactly what is going on with you. When we fail to dissolve inner tensions consciously, all too easily we leak them out *indirectly*, in subtle or not so subtle ways, further down the track. Later in the day suddenly we will feel overwhelmed with irritation in different situations or find ourselves being cynical or sarcastic as we speak with our partner.

Time to Mature

In the beginning there is a challenge in confronting one's own emotional side but the outcome is worth the effort. Soon one appreciates how much lighter life is, how you gradually cease to become entangled in difficulties with others. If you do find yourself in emotional situations, now you will have more insight into what is going on; life is not a disaster, instead a wave of emotional past has flooded into the present. And to have the awareness of what is happening can act as a tremendous relief, because you suddenly take some distance from the situation. You are able to be more of an observer and less of a participator.

Taking responsibility for one's emotions, which means one's individual past, represents a great step in maturity. When we are emotional we are basically behaving like a five year old in an adult body. And for sure, because of our emotional habits, it is 'easier' to slide into unhappiness and blame everyone else than to consciously work on finding happiness within ourselves. This may sound contrary but it is much easier to be unhappy than it is to be happy. Bringing old unconscious patterns to the surface and transforming them demands effort and commitment. To create happiness and love requires the effort of awareness which, *in the beginning*, can be more challenging than choosing the old option of replaying an emotional pattern or drama for the umpteenth time. With awareness we have the possibility to rise above ourselves and establish alternative forms of communication and expression that support and nourish love.

Chapter 5

SEPARATING LOVE FROM EMOTION

The real truth about love is that love is not accidental. Or lying out of our hands beyond our reach. Love *can be kept alive by separating love from emotion*. When we make a conscious effort to recognize our own emotions, and take responsibility for them, we can easily rise above their destructive potential. We need to develop an awareness of the *very* moment we experience a reality shift, where we suddenly contract, close down and feel disconnected. Usually any emotional reaction we experience will be as a result of something your partner/or another person says or does. For some of us even the tone of voice of another person can be enough to trigger old childhood emotions.

Emotions Potentially Dangerous, not Intrinsically

Emotions are potentially dangerous but not intrinsically dangerous. Emotion, when *recognized for what it is*, is not dangerous. Emotion that is brought from the darkness into the light can give rise to profound healing, as will be mentioned in later chapters. Emotion which is not recognized and operates unconsciously can cause tremendous damage and destruction. Indeed, if we look around the world today we can see that what we have before us is a huge extravagant celebration of emotionality. War and fighting prevail all over the place. Everybody is emotional with everybody else: lovers, colleagues, family, friends, nations, religions. One just has to watch the news or a few television soap operas to see that our reality is a glorious gateaux saturated with overwhelming emotions.

People say the most awful things to each other, storming out of rooms half way through conversations and banging doors behind them. People hit and hurt each other and most of what we see is abusive, violent and uncaring type of behavior. Our films and broadcasts are reflecting the way we relate to each other as human beings. Tragically though, as we view television night after night, we receive the endorsement of, plus the education that, emotional behavior is totally acceptable. We come to believe that it is okay for human beings to have absolute disregard for each other. To carry on in war, fear and abuse is normal, expected and accepted. Basically what we condone, unsuspectingly saying yes to, is that it is perfectly fine for humans to spend their lives unconsciously spreading inner toxins and slowly poisoning the environment around us.

Not to Know You are Emotional is 'Wrong'

As we have mentioned before, emotions themselves are not wrong. We are all carrying wounds (and the unexpressed feelings connected to them) that have been inflicted on us through the unconsciousness of other people, usually parents and people closer to us. And they themselves did not know any better. It is not our fault that we live in a society where it is not appropriate to actually express or share our deeper inner feelings, so from time to time getting emotional *cannot be wrong!* To be full of unexpressed feelings is a sad situation, a potentially explosive situation, but it is not wrong. How can it be wrong? The 'wrongness' of the situation comes from our *not* recognizing our emotional condition for what it is worth. From being unconscious about how our emotional side functions, and how emotions dominate our lives and many of our relationships. We need to acknowledge the reality - that we have many unexpressed feelings stored inside us - and to be aware of the negative role they can play in life. If we do not recognize what is going on inside of us, we leak the tension out indirectly through getting into emotional situations with others. And then we may start to wonder why we are fighting with so many people, and the whole world appears to be set against us.

Unconscious Projection of Inner Pain

When we do not recognize our emotions, we unconsciously project our inner pains and unresolved issues onto a person or a situation outside of us. This event is called 'projection'. The charge, the poison of feelings gone sour that we hold inside ourselves, is displaced outward and put on another person. They are at fault and not us. We do not reflect on our own selves when we are emotional but instead our immediate reaction is to blame another person for the wrong things they have said and done. We make them responsible. We get spiteful and deliberately hurtful, saying unkind unloving words that thirty minutes later we can begin to regret for a lifetime.

Mind Clings to Negativity

The problem with hurtful toxic words spoken during a spate of emotion between two people is that the mind finds it hard to forget the emotional statements; the mind clings to them and turns them over and over asking: is it really so? Did he/she really mean this? Am I really like this or that? Mind clings to negativity. While mind very easily forgets positive uplifting moments, it rarely renounces the negative episodes. One helpful step is to avoid making 'emotional' or charged comments from the sidelines. In a partnership and all dealings with people, we need to be acutely aware of *what* we say, and *how* we say it. Listen to the tone of voice you are using and check that your words are *not* emotionally charged – that through your tone of voice the deliberate intention is to say more than the words themselves.

Learn to recognize when you are leaking emotion through your voice. Learn to resist the temptation of sending comments with a deliberately hurtful sting in them. These act like 'emotional darts' that can trigger your partner's emotions. Avoid making remarks that you know, in advance, are bound to upset or hurt someone. Emotion always comes with a charge so it is easy for you to detect it in your voice and in your body. The other person will 'catch' the negative vibration transmitted from you to them which resonates with their own unexpressed feelings, and stimulates emotion into life.

Do Not Take Others Emotion Personally

If your partner gets emotional, it can be helpful to remember that basically their emotion *is not to do with you*. This recognition does not necessarily make dealing with another's emotion any easier, but it can help you to get some inner distance to the situation; you are not so 'identified', and you can therefore be more understanding and compassionate.

Miguel Ruiz says:

Nothing other people do is because of you. It is all because of themselves. All of us live in our own worlds. When we take something personally we make the assumption that the others know what is in our world, and we try to impose our world on their world. If someone gives you an opinion, don't take it personally, because the truth is that this person is dealing with his or her own feelings, beliefs and opinions. That person tried to send poison to you and if you take it personally, then you take that poison and it becomes yours. But if you do not take it personally, you are immune in the middle of hell. Immunity to poison is the gift of understanding emotion. When you take things personally, then you feel offended, and your reaction is to defend your beliefs and create conflicts. You make something big out of something so little, because you have the need to be right and make everybody else wrong. You also try too hard to be right by giving them your own opinions. (See books section *The Four Agreements*, pages 48-50.)

Do Not Tell Others They are Emotional

Do *not tell your partner that they are emotional*. This is a golden rule 'no no' which will be repeated again. Accusing someone of being emotional can really cause a blow up. When you observe your partner is emotional, it is helpful instead to recognize that whatever is happening is in all likelihood connected to their past, and as lovingly as possible step out of their picture for the moment. Put your entire awareness into your body and make every effort not to get emotional yourself. Avoid getting drawn into the drama with them. Whatever they say or do, remember emotion and ego are speaking, not the heart or being. Feel empathy instead of hostility because we all have an emotional aspect that shows up from time to time.

Observer of Emotional Patterns

When we are emotional, in essence we are temporarily 'out of love', a bit out of order as it were. However there is no reason to doubt love itself. Love is ever-present when our heart is in the right place. When we are emotional but *do not know it* unfortunate consequences can easily follow. When emotional we are driven by forces over which we have no conscious control, and without an awareness of our own emotional aspect, we easily become emotional with other people. And this pattern can work against our own better interests in the long run. The more you are able to be the observer, the witness of your experience and get distance from your emotional patterns, the happier you will be. More able to enjoy life and love in the present. You have to build on that awareness. There is no easy solution; ridding oneself of emotion is an ongoing process of observation using the awareness. Remember not to make yourself wrong, or blame or judge yourself for being emotional. Rather you congratulate yourself for catching yourself in the act and turning the situation around in a positive way.

Be positive; it is much easier to step out of a positive affirming mind than a negative critical mind. You see that emotion is active and you take responsibility. When you see emotion for what it is, you are taking a step back, and instead of getting identified you are taking the power of the event into the being. You experience greater life force as the past is left behind in the distance. The more you can give your power to the being and the body in the present, the less momentum the unconscious emotional patterns will have. You do not deny your emotions, your unconscious part, but you transform unconsciousness into consciousness using the power of the awareness.

Chapter 6

SOURCES OF EMOTION

Since earliest childhood we have had to control and manage our real feelings and keep them to ourselves. Gradually as we grow up we become conditioned *not* to express our feelings, *not* to say what we truly feel. Instead we begin to say what is correct or polite or appropriate in the situation. By the time we are adults we have accumulated unexpressed feelings from several different sources that can later contribute to our emotional states.

Childhood Repression of Feelings

During the formative five years of life we are rarely encouraged to express our true feelings, to be authentic to our inner realities. Instead our parents, schools, and the society teach and instruct us *what* to do and say, what *not* to do and say, *when* to say or do it, when *not* to say or do it. Basically we are taught *how* to behave and conduct ourselves so as to cause least disturbance, *how* to be as invisible as possible. Countless times we had to pretend that we were *not* feeling something, repress our tears of sadness or happiness and swallow our shouts of anger or joy. We end up pleasing others, lose courage, spontaneity and the art of self expression.

As children we require the love and affection of our parents as urgently as we need their food and shelter for our survival. To guarantee continued love, the child ends up becoming politician from very early on, pushing down true feelings, smiling in the right places, saying please and thank you, pleasing everybody in order to receive love. The pains and wounds caused through not expressing childhood feelings are usually stored as memories in the body of an individual. For instance, the experience of inner

37

distress suffered as a result of an absence of parental love or conditional parental love will leave its mark. The tension caused through fear owing to a lack of loving vibrations between parents themselves, or the pain of parental rejection and subjective feelings of desperate 'abandonment' will leave scars.

In time our unexpressed feelings and the wounds associated with them grow to form our 'emotional body' or 'pain body' (see Eckhart Tolle, *The Power of Now*, books section). Our pain body represents all the pains that have accumulated through not giving free range to our feelings. Expressing feelings allows them to flow through and out of our systems. Instead we hold onto and store the feelings and carry the past around with us as if we are travelling with some invisible, yet heavy, baggage.

The childhood conditioning of repressing real feelings becomes a habit, and so continues into adulthood; we become political by not saying what we really feel and need and want. Everyone usually walks around saying superficially 'I am fine!' and doing the right thing by others, while underneath carrying a load of unexpressed pain. Effectively, many of us walk around like little time bombs ticking away waiting to blow up at the 'right' touch or trigger, which can come in different forms; for example, the *tone* of voice of a person, or *what* they say or *how* they say it, that stimulates childhood memories and the unhappiness associated with it into life.

Our senses are very connected to our memories. Smell, taste, touch and sound can act as powerful triggers for our memory bank and in an instant we can find ourselves catapulted way back into the past. We retrieve all the intricate details associated with particular episodes in our lives. The smell of a certain perfume or taste of a certain food, a particular sound, like church bells or a piece of music, a particular quality of touch or a touch in a particular place with which you have associations in the past. Our sensory memories can have positive or negative undertones.

For most individuals the family is usually a great source of emotion during childhood. Sibling rivalry and competition for love, plus parental preferences, can cause scars that end up being a source of painful emotions in the future. In adult life the family often continues to be an ongoing source of emotion because too easily guilt is provoked and we get manipulated into doing the 'right thing by the other' in order to get their approval and love, or to prove our value and worth.

Physical Abuse, Sexual Abuse, Sexual Violation

The body stores and 'holds' the memories of every *psychologically and physically traumatic event* that takes place in the life of an individual. The body stores the fear and the memories plus the unexpressed feelings connected to the subjective experience, as a vibration or frequency in the cells. Every trauma from our first day on earth is recorded by the body. Traumas can also occur during birth or in the womb.

When the feelings associated with any traumatic experience *are released and expressed at the time of the* trauma, the long term influence or 'damage' will usually be substantially less. In cases of sexually abused/violated children, rarely do they say anything to anyone, instead bottle up and repress a tornado of conflicting feelings. If a child is able to express or say something, often the words will not be accepted. It is known to happen that a mother will 'side' with her husband or family member before 'believing' the child, because the implications of accepting the truth are beyond belief.

A woman who has been sexually abused in her childhood is unable to express her confusion openly because more often than not the culprit of the sexual interference is a close family member/friend. And to admit to or speak of the traumatic experience to another person becomes impossible. Often a relative will swear the child to secrecy, extract a promise (offering gifts in exchange) or make a threat to keep the young child silent, forcing them not to acknowledge the whirlwind of emotions and feelings swirling within. Interference does not have to be blatant, personal boundaries can be trespassed through innuendoes in the voice, certain sexually 'charged' vibrations or comments or through greedy sexually invasive looks.

Traumas pass as far as linear time goes, but the memory remains stored and a growing girl enters her sexual life carrying a painful wound that can be a potential source of emotion. In many cases women are known to erase the memory, and superficially completely forget about the episode/s as a survival strategy. Filled with unexpressed feelings a woman then is forced to 'harden' and protect herself in the future. Any man coming close to her, or wishing to make love with her, can easily be a trigger for the buried unresolved past. She might suddenly and unexpectedly feel repulsion, disgust or nausea arise in the here and now, and experience what *actually* relates to the past where previously unexpressed feelings lie. Rage, sadness and pain continue to exist beneath the surface. Due to her recorded cellular memory, a woman can easily find herself unexpectedly in a state of contraction and disconnection. When we are in emotion our experience of love and happiness in the present is lost. If and when emotion arises in circumstances of previous sexual abuse, it is crucial to *be able to recognize the situation* and understand what is actually occuring.

Accumulated unexpressed feelings will have the tendency to repeatedly surface indirectly as emotion during adulthood, again and again causing bouts of unhappiness. Which gives the impression that love is going up and down, whereas in reality it is the *level of emotion that changes*. Remember emotions represent our unconscious aspect and are potentially destructive when we allow them to control us and get the upper hand. Instead, with recognition of our emotion, we can turn the situation around and experience it as a healing or empowering one. There is tremendous value in getting in touch with old unexpressed feelings, and releasing them from the system by giving expression to them - a subject to be covered in more detail later.

Conventional Sex as a Source of Emotion

An additional significant source of emotions, as we become sexually mature and continue into adulthood, is sex. Conventional sex – the kind of sex ninety-nine per cent of us are having – is based on pleasure and peak orgasm. However, the by-product of building up a high charge of excitement is that ultimately tension or a 'charge' is produced and deposited into the system. Later the 'false charge' needs to be discharged or released one way or another (to bring balance to the system) and eventually it may appear in the form of emotions.

Conventional sex can be more accurately described as 'emotional sex', a term coined by Barry Long, spiritual master from Australia. A great deal of tension is produced in the body because *the mind habitually forces orgasm* on the genitals. For most people, they do not think that sex is really sex, unless it is accompanied by orgasm. High levels of sensation and excitement and physical tension are built up to reach the peak, which is followed by a discharge and release of 'tension' downward in a pleasurable local genital orgasm.

The spiritual masters tell us that *when energy moves downward* in the body in discharge, tension is the by-product or outcome. Conversely *when energy moves upward*, as in Tantric sexual practice, the result is silence, contentment and joy. After conventional sex tensions in the system will seek and find outlets for release which explains why sometimes a person can feel a bit 'emotionally charged' afterwards - and the reason why it is common for lovers to have a fight or domestic crisis not long after making love. Clearly, if love had been made, then there would be no grounds for a fight because you feel in love with yourself, and with the other person. If there is not a fight with the partner, it is possible that sooner or later you find yourself unexpectedly angry about something else, and finding fault in others for no real reason. Many people report to us that when they truly examine the period of time *after* orgasm they observe that they do experience a sense of disconnection, separation and loneliness.

Sharing of a man about experience of ejaculation causing emotion:

On about the 4th day of the Making Love Retreat I felt a pain in my genitals together with a strong feeling of pressure, similar to the pain I experienced in the past when I have not ejaculated for a longer period of time. At the same time I have to say that I had the feeling my partner and I, during the previous days, had made love in a 'cool' way, not getting very 'hot' or excited, as you suggested to us. So I was sure that I had not got too excited or deliberately repressed my ejaculation, which as you explained, can also cause pain in the testicles and groin area. On the fifth day we talk while we are making love; while I am inside her, I say that I could simply put an end to the pain and ejaculate. In that very moment my penis started to get smaller and smaller and – something that has never happened to me before – slipped out her vagina. 'Ok,' I said to her. Losing my erection is a sure signal that says to me I must not 'come'. The pain and the pressure disappeared again. The next day an orgasm happens to me without me going for it or heading towards it. The orgasm is beautiful because we are experiencing it consciously. Only later, however, I realize a pattern of mine as I suddenly start teasing my beloved, provoking her and making cheeky comments. She tells me she has the feeling I am putting out my stings and that I am pushing her away from me. The realization starts very slowly and it takes me a while to see that I felt lonely after orgasm, and separated from my beloved after so many beautiful days together. For the first time it is obvious to me that I am often emotional after ejaculation. Suddenly it is so clear to see. Even though the experience of the orgasm was good, I was slightly emotional afterwards.

Mind as a Source of Emotion

Mind itself can be a powerful source of emotions. Many people get themselves into obsessive *thinking* and *worrying* so as to produce a state of ongoing anxiety and suffering. Obsessive dwelling on a subject or situation can cause a person to become extremely emotional and unhappy. Perhaps you have had experiences where you were feeling happily contented when suddenly you fall into remembering a disturbing incident from the past. It is most likely that your happiness evaporates in an instant! Or if you think obsessively about a certain problem you may have with a person, you can heat yourself to boiling point in a handful of minutes. Or repeatedly, you upset yourself by telling the same story or drama to your friends again and again. Each time you do this you are recycling those old emotions through your system, every time you are a little bit angry or sad many long years after the event itself. Past becomes difficult to leave in the past.

Many of us are 'identified' with the past and the emotion it carries, so we also begin to define ourselves by our unhappiness, which can make it very difficult to step into the present where life is actually taking place – here and now. Some people are continually harping on about their sad unhappy childhood which messed up their lives, but the fact is there is nothing that can be done to change the past now. One's past has to be accepted, and dealt with in a constructive way. Complaining for the next fifty years is not going to help the quality of life at all. Past and future always involve our minds which are endlessly caught up in thoughts, something that does not exist in the now. Some people can at times appear to be 'addicted' to the emotional state, regularly thinking themselves into states of fear and doubt.

Collective Pains and Emotions

Eckhart Tolle, in his book, *The Power of Now*, chapter 8 (see books section), says emotions usually have a collective aspect as well as a personal aspect. The collective aspect is the pain accumulated in the collective human psyche over thousands of years through disease, torture, war, murder, cruelty and madness. The emotional body or pain body also partakes of the collective emotions. Women also inherit prenatal tensions and traumas from the mother as well as adopting her attitudes toward men in later life.

Every woman has her share in what could be described as the collective female pain body, unless she is very conscious. This consists of accumulated pain suffered by women partly through subjugation of the female, slavery, exploitation, rape, childbirth, child loss and so on over thousands of years. The emotional or physical pain that for many women precedes and coincides with the menstrual flow is the pain body in its collective aspect that awakens from its dormancy at that time, although it can be triggered at other times too. It restricts the free flow of life energy through the body, of which menstruation is a physical expression. Often a woman is 'taken over' by the pain body at that time. It has an extremely powerful energetic charge that can easily pull you into unconscious identification with it. You are then actively possessed by an energy field that occupies your inner space and pretends to be you – but of course, it is not you at all. It speaks through you, acts through you, thinks through you. It will create negative situations so that it can feed on the energy. It wants more pain, in whatever form.
Eckhart Tolle

Chapter 7

DEALING WITH EMOTION – GOLDEN RULES

The crucial question is 'What can I do when I recognize I am emotional?' Recognizing emotion is the easy part, but what can be done to remedy the situation? How should I handle it? How do I return to connection from the disconnection I am experiencing now? How do I find love again?

Five Necessary Steps to Transforming Emotion

There are five essential steps to be taken to dissolve the emotion so that you can extract yourself from the conflict/situation with your partner.

1. Recognize you are emotional (as mentioned in an earlier chapter).
2. Admit out loud in three simple alchemical words, "I am emotional".
3. Say, "I am going now because I need some time to myself. I will return later".
4. Actively move your body for a substantial period of time.
5. Return to your partner.

Golden Rule 1: Recognizing Emotion

It takes practice to recognize emotion. As you start to recognize yourself in the list of symptoms in Chapter 2, you begin to notice your emotion more and more easily – and quickly. You become increasingly adept in detecting emotion. There is an inner recognition of where you are at, an understanding of what is actually going on. You are not left in confusion or doubt about yourself.

Knowing about emotionality and how it operates at an unconscious level gives you a new insight into yourself. You have the opportunity to know *where* you are *when* you are, which can be a great a relief. Instead of thinking your life is falling to pieces, you know instead that you are simply emotional! Not that to be emotional is a comfortable experience but at least you know your partner is not responsible for your suffering. The source lies in your accumulated unexpressed feelings lying in the past. As soon as you start to keep an eye on your changing level of emotion, your ups and downs, you will observe in your relationships with others that disturbances happen less and less often.

Golden Rule 2: Acknowledging Out Loud

We need to externalize the inner recognition of emotion. We absolutely need to acknowledge the situation by saying "I am emotional." No other words will have the same effect, and no other words should be substituted. Words like 'time out' or I need some 'space' do not actually acknowledge what you are feeling, so they do not work as substitutes. We speak the words out loud and clear as we say "I am emotional". Definitely we do not shout and scream these words in an emotional fashion at the poor partner! You simply declare what is going on in your inner world by admitting you are emotional.

Emotion, as mentioned in chapter 2, is an aspect of the ego so admitting to emotion can be a very challenging step to take when you find yourself in the midst of it. In fact, when we are emotional these three particular words will seem to be the most difficult words to say because you feel convinced that you are right!

The ego, which lies directly over the heart center will effectively obscure the heart and the love naturally experienced there. In emotion the *very last thing* the ego will want to do is to give in, to step down from its proud position. The ego never likes to be wrong, or to verbally admit that the other person is not at fault or to blame for the situation. The mind will do its very best to convince you in numerous ways that you have *every* right to blame the other person because they *actually did* something. Ego is very self-centered, it thrives on being right, so to give up this position of false power is usually a humbling experience for a person.

Saying "I am emotional," clearly implies that you have taken responsibility for your emotions. In saying so your partner is absolved, you basically let your partner off the hook. They are removed from the picture as a by-product of your realizing that you are caught up in the past, in emotion. The partner will usually experience a sense of relief. Now *they* know that *you* know what is going on! These three words will act like a sword cutting through layers of unconsciousness. In the moment you speak them out aloud you will feel a big shift in the atmosphere as the level of tension decreases.

Golden Rule 3: Separating to be Alone

After you have admitted you are emotional it is essential to separate physically from your partner. Tell them you are going away now because you need some time to yourself and you will be returning later. Do not slam the door behind you as you leave, this is emotion speaking! Be as loving and polite as possible in the circumstances. If they want to continue the argument, do not answer back, instead tell them that you need to leave the room. And that you will return again soon. Remember, the tendency of emotion is to continue arguing and discussing and getting deeper and deeper into hot water (see indicators of emotion list). By removing yourself physically you avoid the possibility of getting drowned in even more emotions as you continue fighting and hurting each other.

You will need to find a private space, another room in the house, the garden, the forest, or whatever is available to you. Do not drive away in the car in fit of emotion! Driving under the influence of emotion is very dangerous and serious accidents can happen. Stay where you are and do the best you can in the given circumstances.

Golden Rule 4: Get Physical Consciously

Move your body! Consciously, with awareness and with intention. Not mechanically and automatically. Actively move your body for a good period of time. Get breathing! When we are in emotion we need to encourage the toxins moving through the connective tissue (fascia) *out of the body*. Being physically active is crucial to burning up and transforming emotions. It is important to understand that when we are emotional we have effectively departed from the body, even though we also experience the emotion intensely on a body level. In reality we are caught up in an old movie. Our identification with the past removes us from the physical body in the present, where good inner sensations prevail.

Movement of the body is necessary to shift the poisons of unexpressed feelings out of the system. Strong, energetic, conscious, all consuming movement is recommended, for a sustained period of time, not just a few minutes. You will know when your emotion is burned up because you will begin to feel more like your normal self. Making a sound using the voice, combined with active movement, is also good. At times the presence of children or neighbors can be an inhibiting factor, but they should not prevent you from expressing yourself. Find a way that works for you without disturbing all those around you! Place a pillow over your mouth as you scream to dampen the sound. If it is not possible to make sound, moving the body only will have equally beneficial effects.

How to be physical:
Stamp your feet
Dance wildly to music using your legs and arms

Shake your body, arms, hands and head erratically

Start speaking gibberish (unintelligible meaningless talk)

Jump up and down with your arms held up in the air. Shout hoo! each time your two heels hit the ground

Pummel a *thick* pillow or mattress with your fists and have a good belly scream

Jog vigorously for a few miles

Any physical work provided you use your body in a powerful way

Active Dynamic Meditation designed by Osho available on CD

Absolutely avoid lying down when you are emotional even though it may be tempting. When we are emotional we tend to collapse, feel weak, and the more inviting solution to dealing with our emotions is to curl up in bed or watch TV, read a book or have a smoke. Basically when we do so, we continue along in an emotional state, feel sorry for ourselves and nurse our emotions for a few hours. Because of the contracted weakened state it is a challenge to find the motivation to move an inch, let alone to move the body strongly for an hour or so. However the step has to be done and the sooner one gets moving, the sooner the experience of well-being returns.

The more you move your body, the more rapidly the toxins burn up and leave your system. Occasionally it can happen that while you are beating a cushion, for instance, you come in contact with a layer of powerful feelings many layers deeper than your more superficial emotional reaction. Suddenly you start weeping from a central core place in yourself as you connect with old pains/wounds from much earlier years. In other words a flood of previously unexpressed feelings come to the surface for release. And in reality this is precisely what we wish for. We want to get down to the layer of feelings that have been stored inside, unexpressed and poisoning the system, causing emotions in life.

If tears and sadness take possession of you stay with the unfolding process. Allow the tears; don't hold anything back. *And do not try to understand the source or root of the emotion.* Thinking and analyzing brings you into your mind and thoughts and distracts from the experience that is actually happening. Surrender to what is emerging from a cellular level in your system. Healing follows as a by-product of releasing old and buried feelings. Stored memories can be released from the body, in the here and now, by a person getting in contact with the *original feelings hiding at the core* of the emotion.

Transforming old emotions into true original feelings can heal wounds of the past (in the present) on a cellular level. When we consciously turn old emotions into genuine feelings and release them by 'living' them we become whole and healthy again. An old wound in our psyche is healed; the 'poison' of the unexpressed feelings has been discharged; unlived feelings have been expressed, and the system is revitalized. Expressing pent up feelings consciously is a powerfully healing experience.

Golden Rule 5: Returning to Your Partner

After a period of body movement you are likely to notice that you begin to feel a great deal better, and you can view your situation with more lightness and distance. The negativity, and with it the identity, has been burned up through physical expression, and you are able to return to life in the here and now. And to love as well.

When you feel you have done enough movement to burn up your emotion, sit silently for a few minutes to calm down, and begin to tune into your body. Perhaps you notice that you feel your heart again; you are not consumed by negative poisonous thoughts about the other. Perhaps you even feel love and gratitude. Keep your awareness in your body until you reach a point that you feel more grounded and centered in yourself.

When you feel ready to meet your partner again, slowly approach them, and offer them an embrace by opening your arms to them. There is no need to speak right now, or to explain or justify what has happened. Let the past go. Unless of course you want to tell them that you are *not* emotional now and laugh at yourself!

You can use an 'eye' check as you return as a monitor of where you are at in terms of your level of emotion. Allow your eyes to meet the eyes of your partner. Notice if you can meet their eyes. If the answer is yes, you know you have moved through, because before, during emotion, it was probably impossible to have eye contact (one of the symptoms of emotion).

It may sometimes happen that when you do finally return to your partner, you find that you still *cannot* look them directly in the eyes. The sense of separation continues to be in the air. Not the great divide that was there before, you do feel slightly closer to them, but still not fully connected. As if you can now see over the wall that is separating you, but it is not yet completely down. The feedback of only being 'halfway there' is a signal that you will again need to separate, and have another session being physical. And you continue with the movement until you feel that the sense of separation has dissolved. The process takes as long as it takes. The more you follow the Golden Rules, step by step, the process will get shorter and shorter, and more easily you find yourself returned to inner equilibrium, and to love.

Aim of the Golden Rules

Remember: See, Say, Separate, Move, Return!

As emotion is transformed into feeling, through getting physical or actually expressing true feelings (for example tears expressed from the heart, and not tears of self pity), the 'negative' charge is gradually taken out of the wound. This represents a positive step because we gradually cease to identify with childhood events that previously may have haunted us.

When we allow our withheld feelings there is a 'sweet pain': the pleasure of relief as we let go of tensions and inner pressures we have been carrying for years. This is the true aim of the Golden Rules: we want to reconnect with the old unexpressed feelings to heal the past, and turn the present into an experience of sustained love and joy, without being disturbed by emotional upheavals.

Personal sharing of couple:

After we came home from the Making Love Retreat we had a tennis match in a mixed double tournament. We knew that our opponents' tennis skills were about equal to ours which meant we would have to play good tennis to win. Very often in the past in a situation like this we got emotional during the match and we infected each other. Usually we lost the match because of getting emotional! It was more a fight in our own team and therefore we usually lost the real fight in the tennis game.

Now we have learned how to keep the emotions out of the situation, we have discovered how we can challenge our opponents together. We won this match with losing only one single game! And moreover we won all the following matches and won the whole tennis tournament in our mixed doubles club just because each of us were with ourselves, and let the emotions stay out of the match, which enabled us to meet the challenge jointly. By the way, this also helps each of us also when we play in singles matches!

Personal sharing of woman:

Making love more often, in the Tantric way taught by you, has made us into peaceful human beings – no more fighting in the office, which we did daily before we learned from you. And if we do fight, we know that we are not taking enough time for making love. Unfortunately sometimes we are so performance driven and responsible for our company, that we have difficulties to make love a top priority. It was amazing how few times we had to go jogging or screaming before we recognized being emotional quickly enough to stop the fighting (only a total of about five times). We are used to recognizing patterns between us so that helped.

Chapter 8

SCENARIOS SEPARATING LOVE FROM EMOTION

The Process Takes as Long as it Takes

How long does it take to get over a wave of emotion? Basically, there is no time frame for how long you will need to get over your emotions. In the beginning it can take a couple of days or maybe only a few hours. But what is certain is that once you begin to take responsibility for your emotions by naming them out loud, and then dealing with them, the time interval between emotions triggered and emotions getting resolved slowly shrinks.

Couples often tell us that they needed to follow the instructions set out in the Golden Rules only a handful of times before their awareness of emotional states was heightened. With the new understanding they were able to separate love from their destructive emotions. Sometimes conflicts that would normally take them days to process are over within the hour. They report a more relaxed loving rapport between them. The importance of taking emotion out of love is that we are able to protect love, not unintentionally destroy it again and again. We can honor love in the present, and keep it free of contamination or disturbances from the past. Now we are in a position to preserve love in its purity and, using 'the awareness', we can consciously separate the past from the present.

Possible situations that may arise:

Scenario One: You get emotional
Scenario Two: You and your partner both get emotional
Scenario Three: One partner gets emotional, the other does not
Scenario Four: You think your partner is emotional

Scenario Five: A person (other than partner) gets emotional

Scenario One: You get emotional:

As soon as you recognize that you are emotional, follow the Golden Rules explained in the previous chapter on how to transform emotion. In short you begin by saying 'I am emotional', then separate and get your body moving before you return to your partner in due course.

Scenario Two: You and your partner both get emotional:

Usually when one person gets emotional, the other will also become emotional at almost exactly the same time. Each one of us has probably had this experience countless times. The two scenes will happen almost instantaneously as one follows the other in a flash. One partner gets triggered and as a direct consequence the other person also gets involved. For the person who gets emotional first, there is usually no time to intervene and acknowledge their own emotional state.

Remember, emotionality spreads very fast because its toxins are infectious. Remember that, like you, the other person carries a load of unexpressed feelings/emotions too. These get activated by the toxic vibration of the charge carried in your emotions, and trigger the emotions lying latent and unexpressed in the other person. Both people becoming emotional simultaneously can open the floodgates to a torrent of abusive interchanges (verbal and physical) as heaven turns into hell in the interim.

When you are both emotional, *both* follow the Golden Rules, *both* say 'I am emotional'. Then physically separate and go to different places in the house/garden, become active, release and burn up your emotional charge. Or get in touch with your deeper unexpressed feelings, and allow them flow through you, and follow the process through to a satisfactory and loving end.

Scenario Three: One partner gets emotional, the other does not

In this scene one partner is able to hold their ground and remain in the present, unmoved by the emotional wave of the other. They are able to 'hold the space', able to remain loving and supportive. They recognize emotion is active in the other and are not affected by it. They do not take it personally, and consciously do not get caught up in the emotion of the other. If a person has previously worked on discharging their own unexpressed feelings (body of emotion or pain body) it can be that there are no longer reactions triggered in the present moment.

When one partner remains centered and conscious and does not unconsciously slip into emotions, an opportunity for profound healing is created. When there is no answering emotional reaction from the partner, the emotional person can be forcefully thrown back onto their inner selves. As the saying goes, it takes two to tango. You cannot tango alone. There is only a fight if there is someone to fight with. When there is no answering reaction to the projection outward (the blaming or accusing for instance) that same energy is inverted, and like a mirror one sees oneself, reflected for real. In this intensity a window for healing opens. The possibility arises to dive into a deeper layer in oneself where many buried feelings lie. As part of the healing process it can happen (but it shouldn't be expected) that a very clear memory of an actual childhood event flashes through you. In the depth of sadness and pain there can be vivid images relating to a specific happening in childhood. For example, the very first occasion you had a subjective experience of abandonment in your childhood where you were unable to express your fears and feelings related to your parents not ever coming home again. Abandonment is a very common emotion triggered between couples, and feelings of abandonment can recur as a theme throughout a person's life. When the earliest feelings connected to the initial abandonment experience are released and healed through expression, then an individual will begin to be free from the recurring emotional issues around abandonment.

When we contact the root of the injury in a spontaneous way, and allow the pain and tears to flow, we are healed on a mind, body and heart level. Through cleansing the past out of the system, we will discover that the very same issue, when it next arises, will not have the same hold. There is a feeling of detachment. You no longer hold the old pain inside; it has been discharged from the system and is no longer available for reactivation in the form of emotion.

Scenario Four: You think your partner is emotional

Take note again, it is much easier to recognize the emotions of your partner than your own! As a general rule, *never* tell your partner that they are emotional. Simplest is to keep out of your partner's business and instead take care of your own. Make sure you are not getting emotional because they are getting emotional. Telling someone they are emotional, when they are in fact emotional, is like adding fuel to the fire; the situation flares up and takes a turn for the worse.

If you do not tell your partner they are emotional how can you actually help them?

Deep down an emotional person is always longing for love, no matter what the trigger for the emotional outburst may be and no matter how many barriers they put around themselves to keep you away. In emotion we move into a state of fear, and fear reflects the absence of love as already mentioned in chapter two.

In our couple seminars we have often verified the fact that fear is the absence of love. We ask, 'When you are emotional, what are you longing for at the very deepest level?' The word, 'Love!' resounds around the room.

The tragedy is that when we are in an emotional state we are not very loveable! As soon as we express our true feelings we immediately become more innocent and childlike and easy to love.

Stay loving and present. The confirmed truth that an emotional person needs love means we need to be loving to them! The best medicine for emotional symptoms is a big dose of love – simple, sweet, easy. It may happen that your love is not received right away, but if you remain patient, innocent and full of heart, love is an eternally healing force. Do not react to your love not being received at first. If your partner initially rejects your attempts to make contact, watch out that you do not get emotional too because your love has been rejected! Getting emotional can happen all too easily in these circumstances because you are carrying your own personal rejection wounds.

Let your heart guide you. There is no recipe for how to approach an emotional person. Sometimes words like, 'Is there something I can do for you?' or 'Is there something you need?' will open closed doors, but not necessarily. Out of context, any suggestions or formula will sound superficial. Be guided by instinct and a loving heart. How would *you* like to be approached if you were in the situation? Loving, caring touch can be a bridge to reach an emotional person. Sometimes silence is better than words; sit silently next to them, relax into your body, being and heart; embrace them with your presence.

Scenario Five: A person (other than partner) gets emotional

Emotions pop up between all kinds of people, not only between lovers. Friends, relatives, siblings, employees, colleagues, bosses, strangers; the list is endless. On a practical level the easiest way to bring about a change in dealing with emotions and feelings, is to begin with the person closest to you. It can be a vision that you hold in common to increase the vibration of love between you. You can consciously experiment together, and follow the Golden Rules of separating love from emotion, step by step, through to meaningful conclusions. Naturally, these steps will have to be taken several times to get the knack of it.

However, with any other person in your circle, or strangers, dealing with emotions when they arise can be more challenging because they do not have the same understanding as you do. If their emotionality triggers yours, then they won't have a clue what's going on if you start claiming you are emotional. Even so, something has to be done to break the unconscious cycles of emotion running through our lives. Too much unhappiness follows in its wake.

Withdraw yourself. If someone gets emotional with you, or you with another person, it is best to leave their company. Remove yourself as politely and as gracefully as possible, and with haste. Avoid getting into discussion, justification or arguments. You can simply acknowledge that you are emotional, and that anything you say in this moment is unreliable. And that you need some time alone! Even if they do not comprehend what you mean by this. It may not be possible or easy at the office to get physical and work out the negative effect of any emotions. Even so, you can have a quick brisk walk outside, or go to the bathroom and shake your limbs, jump around. When you get home you can do a more thorough workout if you feel some tensions remain in your system.

Wait to speak to the person concerned only when you no longer feel emotional. Give yourself time to get over the emotions. Hopefully, by the time you meet the other person will also have cooled down. Without emotion and our unconscious reactions, constructive communication is more likely to take place. The fight only stays alive if two people are involved. So if you keep an eye on your emotionality, and keep the level down, you will probably be able to solve difficulties more easily and have fewer conflicts with people.

Getting Straight to the Core of the Matter

Many psychotherapists attend our Making Love seminars and after our presentation on emotions and feelings several have come up to us looking a little aghast. They tell us that they spent years studying psychology to get to the central point that we have managed to wrap up in about 90 minutes. The core issues that most of us face are all dealt with in such a practical, simple, uncomplicated way.

Some people, when they hear this revolutionary reorientation on emotion, think it is too simple. Resolution of problems is necessarily arduous, painful work. The mind loves far away solutions and something simple and instant is dismissed as being a bit childish. Only practice gives rise to a body of experience, and separating love and emotion is definitely something to be experienced in order to reap its benefits. Talking about the pros and cons of the approach is worthless. Getting down to understanding emotion and taking responsibility for this aspect of ourselves, lifts people out of the domain of difficulties and problems.

Some people explain our emotional 'attacks' as a function of the 'inner child', which continues all through life to be wounded and injured by childhood experiences. At times when the inner child is at play, unconscious emotional behavior is excused or condoned or accepted as part and parcel of the personality. It is okay to be expressing the inner child, hurting other people now because mummy did not give me enough love way back then. But the real question is; how long do we want to cling to our childhood, and the pain of it all? We have to move on and become adults so that we can create a more harmonious loving environment for ourselves in the present. For years we may find the same inner child issue replayed, yet there is no resolution. As long as we give the inner child the thumbs up, our okay, we give our unconscious emotions free range.

Recognizing the inner child is an important step on the way to growing up but it is not the whole picture. The hurt inner child has to begin to take responsibility for the past, and resolve the emotions accumulated there, and to see how past wounds repeatedly destroy the present. The child is now an adult. The next step is to accept that the inner child exists, and at the same time to avoid using the inner child concept when you go into emotion. Begin to view the phenomenon on the level of emotion and emotionality. View it as past and present, *and the attempt to keep the past out of the present.* Intentionally separate love from unconscious emotion and deal with any unexpressed feelings as a conscious side issue. As we have mentioned before, taking direct responsibility for emotions represents a step in maturity as a human being.

In fact, in our seminars we tell couples that the information on emotion and feelings is very dangerous information because *now we know* the route to happiness. We cannot blame others or circumstances anymore; we have instead to resolve the past and unexpressed feelings lying there. If we begin to deal with emotions *as* emotions they begin to burn up and gradually our identification with them reduces. In time you discover situations that used to trigger emotion in you produce no disturbance now, you can smile and move on in love. From inner child who can be emotional, demanding, needy or self-righteous, we have to return to the *innocent* child, who is adorable, irresistible and charming.

Chapter 9

BEGIN TO EXPRESS FEELINGS

Express feelings as you feel them. Recognizing and working through old emotions is only half of the solution to our emotionality. The other half is equally important which is to begin to express feelings – in the here and now! Learn to express feelings in the *very* moment they arise. We must express our feelings in order to avoid accumulating more emotion which we now realize will backfire on us sooner or later. We are not encouraged to express our feelings since childhood so we have to learn the art of it, and get to the heart of it. We need the courage to look into ourselves, to be honest and to show our vulnerable side, our weaknesses, our insecurities, our sadness. When feelings are expressed in the moment to which they belong they are 'pure' and do not have the weight and toxic charge of emotion lying behind them. Feelings can be expressed in a light, playful and innocent way without hurting anyone else.

Acknowledge by Saying 'I Feel'

Remember, on the level of feelings we talk about our inner selves, in contrast to emotion where usually we talk about the other person. Be certain that you are not blaming your partner indirectly by saying ' I feel you always...' or 'I feel you never...'. In feelings we acknowledge what we feel by saying 'I feel that...' If we can leave the tendency to blame other people to the side, we are more easily able to connect with our feelings and inner truth.

Use Words or Body

To keep life and love free of emotion we must begin to express feelings as they arise through words or through the body. Often verbal communication about what you feel may be sufficient. But at other times you might need to move your body. It is great to follow any urges of the body, to jump and leap around. Use your body to express the inner feeling. Just move! Don't sit still and repress any impulses to move. Get the feeling through and out of your body as soon as possible. Do not hang onto your feelings for an instant, unless you are in a hopelessly inappropriate situation. Move with the rising feeling and don't let your mind talk you out of it. Allow the tears to flow; the roar to express itself; jump up and down; do something fast.

When you express what you feel from the heart, without any blame or underlying emotion, then your words speak directly to the heart of the other person. Anything expressed from the heart resonates in the heart of the other, and they will suddenly become receptive and responsive to you.

Express Feelings as They Rise

When we are able to catch feelings of anger, sadness, despair or frustration at their very root, in the exact moment when they arise within us, they do not have a long life span – eight seconds or so. This eight seconds is an insight from Barry Long, and we personally have found it to be true in our own experience - many times. Anger, when caught in the very instant it flares up, can completely dissolve with one deep long roar. Sadness or pain arising from the depths of the being, if allowed, will flow through you simply, gently and quickly, with refreshing and uplifting effects.

Hard and Fast Rules About Expressing Anger

Another golden rule! When you practice consciously expressing anger there are a few rules that come with it, and these are not to be broken under *any* circumstances. If you feel anger, do *not* direct it on your partner, even if on the surface your emotions are convincing you that he or she is at fault. Do *not* touch your partner or do *anything* to physically hurt their body – do not even face them. Turn and face in the opposite direction with your back to them, and allow a deep roar to emerge from your belly.

Source of all Anger is Sexual Frustration

Barry Long, a modern day enlightened authority on human spirituality and sexuality, and to whom we have previously referred, informs us that *all* anger is a result of sexual frustration. Our personal observations during the many years of researching and exploring sex have confirmed that he speaks the truth. Sexual frustration, the lack of sex, the absence of fulfilling sex, gives rise to unexpressed anger in men and women. And sexual frustration exists because of an innate longing to dissolve into blissful union with another, and ultimately with the whole of existence. We do not know how to enter sex in a way that creates an ecstatic circle of love and vitality, how to express our higher sexual potential as human beings.

After conventional orgasm most people tell us that there is no genuine feeling of satisfaction or completion on an inner level. Instead people can easily feel lonely or abandoned or sad or disconnected or drained. Sexual disappointment accumulates as the years pass by and the frustration is stored becoming a potential source of emotion. (See *The Heart of Tantric Sex*, Chapter 10, Diana Richardson.) In many life situations we are easily provoked and leak out sexual unhappiness in the form of anger, irritation, impatience and restlessness.

If you observe that you are a person who gets angry easily, this is perhaps a signal that indicates the need to consciously begin to express accumulated unexpressed anger. To do this, take some time to yourself in a room alone and get your body moving by beating on a big pillow or mattress. Go with your body, movement, and sound (as suggested in chapter seven) for an hour or so.

Express sadness; allow the tears. Sometimes it is possible to transform anger into its opposite of underlying sadness. Sadness when expressed from its root is not a prolonged 'sorry for myself' weep, but instead a profound heart rending expression of sadness. The tears and pain pass on quickly, leaving you feeling refreshed and alive. Sometimes, though, several hours are absolutely necessary to unburden yourself of tears and sadness, perhaps with the feeling that you are weeping for the whole of humanity. It is possible that you may have to go through this a few times before you feel completely emptied out of unexpressed sadness and sorrow. After such experiences you will always feel lighter, expanded and fresh, more connected to people around you. Emotions bring darkness and separation. When you honor and express your feelings you create light and love.

Express Your Love, Share Your Love

Most novels and films are about the pain and tragedies of not getting the love we want. Very little is portrayed about joyful, fulfilling, uplifting aspects of love. Life and love would be much richer if we would tell each other how much we love each other, and not hold back in egotistical fear of vulnerability and exposure. Each time you express your love or be more loving to a person, the vibration of love in and around you strengthens, expands and spreads through your life. You become a loving, generous person and not an unpredictable emotional person.

Not expressing feelings, even of love and appreciation, also quickly turns sour when repressed! After not saying how you feel you may observe that you feel a bit disconnected or depressed some minutes or hours later. Say, I love you, share your love, don't be miserly with love. Love is an intrinsic quality that we are born with. And what we need to do is create a passage for our love to flow – to all people that we meet along life's journey, not only to the people nearest and dearest to us. When we walk down the street we should be radiating love to the whole universe, and not holding ourselves small, in contraction and fear of others. When we are in fear, we slowly lose touch with our essence - which is love.

Make sure you are not feeling sorry for yourself! If while you are crying or expressing yourself you *also* feel a victim of your situation, like 'poor me!' this is a sign that you are still basically emotional: not really in touch with the core of your unexpressed feelings. Sometimes, the mind will go over the sad story again and again and floods of tears will accompany each excursion into the painful past. But this kind of release is not necessarily a deep cleansing or healing experience. It is still on the level of emotion and afterwards a sure sign will be that the person does not feel refreshed or any better at all. Often they will be swollen-eyed and exhausted after hours and hours of crying. When tears are expressed from the core level of the being, the eyes are usually shining and the person is softly radiant in their vulnerability.

Dealing with Jealousy

Common emotional experiences are anger, frustration, impatience, sadness, jealousy, abandonment, unworthiness, feeling the victim of situation, sensitivity to criticism or feedback and constantly seeking affirmation. Jealousy, however, is perhaps the most debilitating and excruciating of emotions, experienced by men and women alike. Jealousy is not an expression of love for that person as we so easily assume. Jealousy comes out of a fear of losing a person. Jealousy is concerned with possessing and controlling another person, and not granting them the right to live their life. Jealousy has its roots in comparison, and women in particular are taught to compare themselves with each other, with special focus on beauty, body and sexual attractiveness. Comparison is a useless activity of the mind because each individual is unique and incomparable. When we are jealous we do and say extremely unconscious things that can have negative consequences. When jealous, try to physically burn up the toxic jealousy that has overtaken you. Once the understanding that love resides within you settles into an experience jealousy can begin to dissolve, but it is like a virulent weed that needs quite some extracting before it finally loses power.

Meditation to Transform Jealousy, Anger, Sadness, Hatred and Possessiveness

Don't repress it, express it. Sit in your room, close the doors, bring your jealousy into focus. Watch it, see it, let it take as strong a flame as possible. Let it become a strong flame, burn into it and see what it is. And don't from the very beginning say that this is ugly, because that very idea that this is ugly will repress the jealously, will not allow it total expression. No opinions. Just try to see the existential effect of what jealousy is, the existential fact. No inter-pretations, no ideologies. Just let the jealousy be there. Look into it, look deeply into it and so do with anger, so do with sadness, hatred, possessiveness. And by and by you will see that just by seeing through things you start getting a transcendental feeling that you are just a witness; the identity is broken. The identity is broken only when you encounter something within you.

Osho, transcribed teachings, Tao: The Pathless Path

Person in the Present has 'Hurt' You in the Past

A situation such as this can be delicate. When you are in a relationship it can be that some months or years ago this same person acted unconsciously or against your personal interests to which you had an emotional reaction. What can I do today if they do something similar again and all the emotions from the first time overwhelm me? It is most helpful here to recognize that ultimately it is *your* emotion and you cannot make them respon-sible for your reaction. If you had expressed your real feelings related to the incident *at the time when it was actually happening*, the truth is you would be carrying less of an emotional charge today. The charge would have been released and cleansed from the system because you fully expressed your associated feelings at the appropriate time.

When and if a similar situation arises again it will be fresh in the sense that the feelings are not pre-contaminated *by the earlier unexpressed feelings.* When there is an accumulation of emotion the charge gets more toxic and forceful. Whenever there is a conscious release of emotion, the load and the internal pressure is reduced. Your triggers become less active and the past is left in the past as you become available to the unfolding present moment.

Life Free of Emotion Between Couples

It is possible with commitment and a bit of practice to live a life free of emotion. Personally, we would go so far as to say that a life free of emotion is highly desirable: an orientation that can change the quality of a person's life. It is not that we can manage a life free of emotion with all people in our lives, but with our partner we definitely can have an emotion-free life together. With friends and other people sometimes the difficulty is that they do not view the situation in the same way as you do. Strangers and friends do not have the orientation in emotions that you have, and you certainly cannot start raving to them about unconscious emotional states! Many people do not understand why they are so unhappy, why love is so difficult to sustain, why they run into conflicts all the time, why friendships are often so short lived. The solution for unhappiness is to learn to put emotions in the right place, and not on others: to take responsibility for your own past and to acknowledge your emotions when triggered by someone in the present.

Emotion can be Addictive

To some of us a vision of life without emotion may sound almost too calm and tranquil, even boring and uneventful. The emotional highs and lows can give a kind of meaning to life; that suffering and experiencing yourself as a victim is your lot. As mentioned earlier, a person can easily get addicted to the intensity of emotion because it is an experience of 'overwhelmingness'. But it is useful to remember Osho's words that "overwhelmingness has no value in itself, it simply shows that we have an emotional personality". Without emotion continually disrupting love, the flow of days, months, and years merge into each other and there is a sense of timelessness; everything is fresh and simple. The relationship is not encumbered by a series of dramas that mark the territory as we move through it, to form a chain of unhappy events that becomes our past.

Emotion Creates Past

In general, when we look back on our relationships, the negative tendency of our minds is to habitually recall the series of difficult and emotional moments. Unknowingly we are dragging them along behind us with each step we take forward. We have grudges, resentments, judgments; we don't forgive each other; we don't show our vulnerability for fear of being hurt; we don't let our love flow; we hold love back and begin to demand love instead. It always helps to remember the words of Osho who says that in the inner world 'the more love you give, the more love you have'.

Emotion can set a chain of reactions into play, which creates karma, and can influence the future in perhaps unbeneficial ways. When our relationships are free of emotion, and filled with love and understanding instead, we are not unconsciously creating difficulties and challenges that may later ricochet back on us and be the cause of unhappiness.

Learning to drop your personal likes and dislikes is a helpful tool given by Barry Long. Notice how your inner world can change according to your likes and dislikes. If you 'like' something you are happy, everything is okay. If you do 'not like' it you get upset or disturbed because things are not going your way. Too many dislikes will cause the level of emotion to rise and fall, and so you end up with a life where everything fluctuates. Likes and dislikes indicate that we identify with a situation. What is required of us is to have a 'choiceless awareness', to stop choosing, to accept the situation *as it is* without getting identified with our preferences. If we want to relax then acceptance is the way. When we deny something *that is* we create inner conflicts and tensions. The more we identify with a situation the greater the unhappiness.

Personal sharing by woman:

The other great thing about your teaching was the difference between emotions and feelings. We are still both working hard at the 'daring to express our feelings' part. I still sometimes don't dare to express them in order to minimize stress when it is already there. But then my resentments toward the stress come out in other ways, in aggressions – so I don't serve the whole if I don't say what I feel! My head knows that, but the little girl inside is still afraid to lose the love she needs so badly.

During our third time of attending your seminar I had a beautiful release inside. A great pain came up in my vagina or uterus shortly before my period, usually I never have that. I had to wake up my husband and ask him to put his penis inside and to keep it lying still. I was hoping some tension could be dissolved, as we have learnt with you about the healing powers of the penis. We started talking about the pain and at one point I said 'I carry this pain with pride.' 'For who?' asked my partner. Instantly I replied, 'for my father, of course.' My husband said 'But your father does not see you, is not interested in you, and thinks that you're crazy anyway!' All of which is true. I realized that the little girl in me still does everything she can to win her father's love, because she was not able to reach him with her great love for him when she was little. So I took my pillow (standing for the little girl) into my arms and finally cried about this. The tears and mourning washed away my core belief that love does not have a chance (because it did not have one back then).

This belief had led to my subtle dismantling of love whenever it showed itself, with a little criticism here and some aggression there. I seem to have done that in order to re-experience the disappointment of not reaching somebody with my love, which was so overwhelmingly big when I was a child and had left me so very lonely. After the crying and recognizing what it was telling me, the pain in my belly slowly went away. I am very careful now to give love a real chance, especially with my husband and children.

Personal sharing by woman:

I connected with my own rejection wound. I have been in it for days – in pain and panic and not able to see my way. It's like a rewinding. Right now I am back to ages seven to eleven, realizing how much this little flower has been abused. I feel compassion for myself, my partner, all the unconsciousness ... from the wounds I have rejected others, especially men. Everything has been about projection, I cried for hours.

Personal sharing by woman:

The wounds seem all to be in the heart – all about receiving love and giving love. When a lot of rejection is there, there is a closing to receiving love and a disbelief that my love has value to a man.

Personal sharing by woman:

Very early in the process I had to let go of this idea and identification that I am a very fucked up and wounded woman. To disengage from the emotional, over and over, is a delight.

Chapter 10

SEX AND EMOTION

Sex Rids Us of Pent Up Tensions

Sex is frequently used to relieve the tension and pressure of our emotions. Sometimes the urge for sex is not to do with sex per se, but the result of a heightened level of emotion. The orgasm, with its downrush of excitement in the form of a pleasurable climax, also acts as a way to unload emotional charge or tension. The orgasm diminishes the degree of emotional tension, like the valve of a pressure cooker, releasing steam from time to time. In chapter 6, on the sources of emotion, we mention sex as one of the contributing factors. Sex can be the source of emotions, and sex can also be used to superficially release emotion. Thus, during sex two processes are involved. On the one hand, due to the high degree of excitement, tension is deposited in the system, which can lead eventually to an increase in the level of emotionality. On the other hand, during orgasm we release tensions that we have previously gathered and stored. Of course we do not build up and release these emotions with intention, they are the by-products of the stimulating, tense style of sex that is practiced in our society. There is no concrete sexual education available and as a consequence we become unconsciously 'sexually conditioned'. We are not aware that as we grow up we are subjected to a mighty invisible influence, and slowly but surely, we become imprinted and shaped by prevailing sexual views. And we then begin to reflect that conditioning or style of sexual behavior for the rest of our lives.

Women as well as men tend to release tensions of emotion during orgasm. But it is perhaps true to say that men do so to a greater extent than women. It is a fact that men ejaculate much more easily and more often than women, who frequently experience difficulties in reaching orgasm. (for further information on female sexuality, refer to *Tantric Orgasm for Women*, Diana Richardson)

Men have Learnt not to Show Their Feelings

Perhaps men are using sex in order to release emotions because they have been conditioned and taught *not* to show their feelings – resulting in a high emotional stress level. Men have as much heart and feelings as women have. Nevertheless there is a tendency to regard tears and vulnerability in a man as a weakness, and those who show their real feelings are viewed as unmanly. The result of this attitude is that men are forced to disregard and repress their true feelings, and to be indifferent with regard to their actual needs and sensitivities.

Male Ejaculation Can Lead to a Negative Form of Relaxation

After ejaculation most men say they experience a type of 'relaxation'. This is so because semen is released (which represents tremendous potency and life force) and the pressure of unexpressed feelings/emotions is temporarily reduced. However, the type of relaxation that men usually describe has nothing to do with true experience of relaxation. What men are usually experiencing is a 'negative relaxation', due to a kind of relief felt in the system after a heavy weight that was being carried has temporarily been offloaded.

What actually happens in true relaxation is the experience of feeling empowered, more vital, more open and loving. It is rare that a man can say he feels these qualities after ejaculation: refreshed and connected in love. It is possible, but it's rare. Instead, many men report that they feel tired, a little empty and alienated, and that they prefer to turn over and go to sleep.

Habitual Unconscious Ejaculation Versus Conscious Ejaculation

Ejaculation as such is not being questioned. Ejaculation is without doubt a pleasurable and necessary biological process. The question here is the 'how' of ejaculation. And it is true to say that most men ejaculate basically out of habit. Ejaculation is experienced as an involuntary, uncontrollable and overwhelming force, over which a man has no command at all.

As with most habits, a habitual pattern reflects a level of unconsciousness. Perhaps it is possible that the restlessness of men, with their sexual drive and desire has more to do with the release of their emotional tension, than with sex as such. A vicious circle of desire and discharge/release is formed, and a person can find themselves caught in an unsatisfying circuit without ever once in their lives experiencing a blessed state of inner completion and fulfillment.

If ejaculation is not done as a matter of routine, but rather as a conscious decision, it will usually *not* have the usual negative by-products. You stay totally relaxed and present; you tell your partner what is happening, and you accompany the experience from moment to moment, relaxing into the sensations without forcing the body in any way. After a conscious ejaculation there can also be an experience of expansion and empowerment.

Women can Absorb Male Tensions

With ejaculation and/or aggressive emotional intercourse a man can without realizing it, deposit the negative vibrations of his emotions in a woman. The disturbed charge is transmitted to the woman because in the male and the female dynamic 'she' represents the container (see *The Heart of Tantric Sex*, and *Tantric Orgasm for Women*, Diana Richardson), as the absorbing and receptive aspect. Any emotional tension that a woman adopts from man will add to her own body of emotion.

Tensions stored in the vagina are able to 'jump-start' ejaculations in a man. Through sexual stimulation (mostly of the clitoris) the woman releases tension in the form of an intense downward rush of sexual excitement that can cause a man to ejaculate out of the blue, unless he is unusually centered and present. Emotional tensions stored higher in the vagina, especially around the cervix area, get activated in the face of strong stimulation and arousal. This tension as it moves sort of 'pulls' an ejaculation out of man. Some men can hardly believe how quickly they come. Some men have described the feeling as a kind of dark cloudy 'force' overwhelming them and there is no option but to surrender. This will explain why so easily a man ejaculates just a few split seconds before a woman reaches her climax.

True Male Authority in Sex

A man discovers his true male authority by focusing on love as a priority, and by keeping emotion out of his sexual expression. In order to burn up stored emotion it is helpful for man to exercise on a daily basis. Over the centuries we have become alienated from our bodies. Most people are sitting at work and hardly ever exhaust themselves physically. The days of hunting and gathering, fetching water and carrying wood are over for most of us. Nowadays, with our limited physical movement, we fail to burn up our accumulating tensions in a natural, physical, regular way.

Instead inner tensions lead to restlessness, the need to always 'do', the inability to relax and remain present to the unfolding moment. For sure it may be more of a challenge to begin to release emotions on a conscious level than to do so through sex. With sex the release is a pleasurable experience, whereas the thought of jogging is not nearly as enticing.

When the level of stress and emotion is reduced, man enables himself to stay more present during sex, which increases his ability to make love for a longer time. He is able to decide consciously when, and if, he ejaculates. It does not happen out of the blue of its own accord. By taking responsibility for his emotions and by keeping them out of sex, a man can rediscover his true male potential.

At first it might look like a big loss not to get a 'reward' in sex; however, whoever takes responsibility gains a new inner freedom – and that is the other side of the coin. With responsibility you gain the freedom to express yourself with intention as opposed to acting out of habit. Instead of being torn by emotions from time to time, you grow into a loving human being. You rise above the cycles of unconsciousness that have been passed down from generation to generation. Life gains a totally new quality when the genitals are used for love, and not purely for gratification.

If the genitals are used exclusively in the service of love, which is actually their higher design and function, then they literally become 'generative organs' and sex becomes an act which generates vitality, as opposed to discharging it. Reproduction is only part of the function of the sexual interaction. With a new understanding of the genitals, in accordance with intrinsic male-female polarity, it is possible to give love a new expression. These are not dreams of the future, but possible in the here and now, and with the person you are together with. You learn to contain the vitality and expand with it, dissolve into it. With taking responsibility for the emotional aspect arises a unique chance to freely determine our sexual encounters without limitations and independent of past experiences.

Tantric Sex Reduces Levels of Emotionality

When a man and a woman begin to make love consciously and begin to avoid 'emotional' sex, there is an immediate and remarkable shift in the emotional state of the woman. She feels herself more open, more loving, more loved, more serene, more content and not so touchy, easy to upset and do the wrong thing by (low grade emotionality). Instead of nagging and complaining and finding fault in her man she feels loving and loveable. Women in our seminars report a shift in their inner world within two or three days of changing the way of making love. Men too report a positive change in their own emotional state: less irritable or restless or aggressive. They feel more centered, more grounded in their bodies, more present and aware, more relaxed and loving.

To be present and not run after orgasms is a more confronting and challenging option because it requires our attention and our awareness. We have to make a conscious, concerted effort. However, there is an urgent need for humans to return to their bodies, and burn up accumulated emotion (as described in the Golden Rules) so that the sexual experience can transform into to a pure and natural expression.

Undetected Emotionality can Lead to Sexual Abuse

Sexual exchange in its purity, free of emotion and excitement, is an absolutely positive healing experience. There exists great confusion as to why sex can be so beneficial and at the same time it is also the source of much anguish and pain. Sex can be beautiful or beastly. How can it be that the very same elements - genitals - can have such differing constellations and expressions? Sex can be seen as a kaleidoscope where each twist of the lens presents totally unique shapes and patterns, but as far as sex is concerned, unfortunately not all views are equally pleasing. It is our personal impression that unconscious, undetected emotionality is responsible for all types of violence, sexual abuse and sexual aggression. The tension of stored repressed feelings can turn into high levels of desire, the craving for sexual stimulation and excitement and discharge. Intense sexual stimulation can also motivate a person's pain body into expression that can easily lead to unhappy endings.

Chapter 11

CHILDREN AND EMOTIONS

Keep Emotion Away from Children

It is highly recommended that parents do not display their emotionality in front of their children. This is perhaps the worst education they can receive. Don't argue and fight when you are in their company, be it driving or eating or whatever activity you are involved in. Resolve the emotional situation with your partner before, if possible, and definitely do not do have an emotional confrontation in front of the children. If it is *not* possible to clear your emotional state before you meet your children be acutely aware that you do not discharge or leak your emotion indirectly on to them. Leaking emotion can happen through displays of irritation and impatience and saying words that have a charge or a sting hidden in them.

Absence of Love Causes Fear

Love is essential nourishment for a child and ranks alongside real food in significance, as mentioned earlier. When there are negative toxic vibrations of emotion between the parents instead of a loving ambience, a child will contract and shrink in fear. The child experiences home as a 'dangerous place'. There will be an inner tension and a loss of relaxation and connection to their innermost essence of love. The child then creates defenses to protect itself and will develop certain strategies to get love or to test love. The process of doing so will usually involve repressing the real feelings, behaving correctly and pleasing others in order to survive, not living a life of spontaneity and joy. The end result can be that the child is needy, time consuming, demanding, and often unhappy. Eventually the child is likely to grow up to be an emotional human being.

Children Imitate Parents' Emotion

Many of us are emotional as adults simply because as children we witnessed and absorbed the negative vibrations of our parents being emotional with each other. We imitate our parents' behaviors, just in the way children tend to imitate how father or mother stands, sits or walks. One example: A while ago we were the only customers in a small Italian supermarket, and we experienced first hand a show of emotional behavior by a young boy where it was absolutely obvious that he was imitating someone. His mother was serving us when he walked in and there was a short interchange between them. Unexpectedly the boy, not more than eight or nine years old, turned on his mother and began gesticulating wildly, screaming and shouting at her in a disrespectful and unloving manner for quite a while. At first the mother stared at him in shock then she tried to get a word in, but quickly gave up. And then she simply let her head hang downcast in shame and silently finished slicing the cheese. What was extremely obvious to us, and no doubt rang as clear as a bell to her, was that the son was behaving exactly like her husband. The son had witnessed the father speaking to his mother many times in an abusive way and was imitating him. Inadvertently, the son had learned from his father the way to communicate with his mother, and thus ultimately all women. No child of such a tender age would ever speak to the mother in this way, the one who represents comfort, love and sustenance unless they had seen such a performance take place in front of their eyes.

Emotion Passed Down the Generations

Through inheriting emotionality from our parents, we unconsciously pass emotional behavior on to the next generations. A child growing up with negative imprints from either parent can be influenced for the rest of their lives. All relationships, especially intimate relationships, will become difficult to sustain. During our seminars couples with children often come and share with us that they feel deeply saddened to see how much emotion they have unconsciously discharged on their children, how unaware they have been about their own unresolved inner feelings. We unfortunately tend to grow up thinking that emotional example we see around us is the appropriate way for humans to communicate and relate to each other.

Children Have Positive Response to Less Emotion

As far as emotion is concerned, it is never too late to start bringing the situation into balance. Parents frequently report to us that as soon as they start to take responsibility for their emotions, the level of harmony and love in the home increases. The children feel immediately that 'love is in the air', that there is an absence of tension or emotional charge between the parents. A child is infinitely sensitive and able to detect the harmony and love between the parents, and relaxes as a consequence of the parents' relaxation. A child is able to recognize love in the eyes of its parents.

Couples from our seminars have the advantage of making love in a relaxed style and with greater frequency, not only once in a while. By making love they find that they support the family ambience indirectly. When love is flowering between them as a couple they shower the children with love and contentment. There is a natural overflow into the rest of life.

Childhood Feelings of Abandonment

A very common issue that most of us carry with us from childhood into adult life is a painful wound of abandonment, already mentioned in a previous chapter. At some time during our first five to seven years of life most of us had the feeling that our parents had abandoned us, had forgotten us, did not love us, and were not ever coming home again. Even if we had the security of shelter and food three times a day, most people have felt that their parents did not have enough time for them, did not love them enough. They were often left alone or passed on to other people to take care of them. From this subjective childhood experience (and therefore one hundred per cent real) many people end up as rejected, wounded beings carrying pain from the past. Ask 50 people if they felt welcomed and truly loved by their parents and usually all of them will say no. We ask this question regularly in our workshops and it is rare that a person declares they felt truly welcomed and loved by their parents; it is rare to find a child conceived with clarity and intention. The unexpressed feelings relating to abandonment and rejection will become obstacles for the rest of our lives. We will feel abandoned by our lover for the smallest of reasons, and the pattern will continue even if we change partners. The feeling of abandonment will continue to surface until we get down to the level of expressing the original pains experienced in childhood.

Personal sharing from a woman:

The information about keeping love and emotion apart helped me greatly over the last few years. I love my children with all my heart. Still I remember very well how I, nevertheless, lost control again and again, and that I yelled at them. Afterwards, I always felt very sorry. The more my husband and I dived into our love making, the more rarely that happened. Today I can hardly remember when it happened the last time. I believe that the yelling at the kids was a discharge of the frustration and the held-back emotions and that it had actually nothing to do with the children. I discharged it there because children are so direct. I realized that my need for changing my husband and criticizing him depends on if we are in the 'making love space' or not. It is as if we dive into another space while we make love. After the love making this space still lasts for some time. It is a space in which I love him with everything that belongs to him. It is like stepping out of duality. I lose the need to judge. And surely it is also because I love myself in that space and that I feel loved with all that belongs to me.

Here is a very sad example of the destructive power of unconscious emotion, from the book *The Four Agreements by Don Miguel Ruiz* (see book section).

There was a woman who was intelligent and had a very good heart. She had a daughter whom she adored and loved very much. One night she came home from a very bad day at work, tired, full of emotional tension, and with a terrible headache. She wanted peace and quiet, but her daughter was singing and jumping happily. The daughter was unaware of how her mother was feeling; she was in her own world. She felt so wonderful, and she was jumping and singing louder and louder, expressing her joy and her love. She was singing so loud it made her mother's headache even worse, and at a certain moment, the mother lost control. Angrily she looked at her beautiful girl and said, 'Shut up! You have an ugly voice. Can you just shut up!'

The truth is that the mother's tolerance for any noise was non-existent; it was not that the little girl's voice was ugly. But the daughter believed what her mother said, and in that moment she made an agreement with herself. After that, she no longer sang, because she believed her voice was ugly and would bother anyone who heard it. She became shy at school, and if she was asked to sing, she refused. Even speaking to others became difficult for her. Everything changed in her because she believed she must repress her feelings in order to be accepted and loved. Whenever we hear an opinion and believe it, we make an agreement, and it becomes part of our belief system. This little girl grew up, and even though she had a beautiful voice, she never sang again. She developed a whole complex from one toxic remark made by the one person who loved her the most: her own mother.

Chapter 12

COMMUNICATION AND RELATIONSHIP SKILLS

It makes a big difference to our lives when we discover there is something that can be done to make love easier. We are not helpless in a situation where we have acted inappropriately or hurt someone unintentionally. We now have a basic tool in our hands - self awareness – to be aware of what happens in our senses and how we are affected in the present. The more clear our senses (relationship to body in the here and now), the more we become aware of *how* we are affected in the present. The clearer our senses, the more likely we are to *give* information and *receive* information as it is, as opposed to acting from the past where our emotions lie. Below are a few suggestions that can be of support in maintaining a harmonious relationship.

1. Intention Behind Your Communication

Be aware of the words coming out of your mouth. Ask yourself, 'Why am I saying this?' 'What am I saying?' 'How am I saying it?' Think before you speak. Look for the intention behind your words. Am I using these words to hurt or to get revenge? What am I saying? Is it my business? Does it relate to now? Is it from the past? What is it I really want to say about what I am feeling? Am I leaking my emotion indirectly on another person in the way I am saying it? Are my words charged with the negativity of emotion, or am I speaking from my heart? Absolutely avoid 'emotional darts', or stinging comments that carry a charge specially designed to provoke. The other person can easily 'catch' the negativity and react to it. As a result you will end up in an emotional drama because of the hidden content in your words. You may feel a little relief through discharging some of your emotion, but it is really at another person's expense because now they have been infected by your negativity. If you notice yourself leaking emotion by sending an emotional dart to your partner, immediately take responsibility by admitting to it.

2. Accept Your Partner as They Are.

You love them the way they are or you don't. Do not try to change them to fit your picture of how the ideal person should be. If you want to relax and stay in love, acceptance is the only way. All denial and non-acceptance creates tension. By saying 'no' to the situation we get tense and emotional; by saying 'yes' and accepting how things are, we can relax and enjoy life.

3. Listen and Speak Through Heart, not Mind

Listen with an open accepting heart to what your partner is communicating to you. Don't be quick to answer back, justify or defend yourself. Continue to stay open and listen instead. Be receptive. Be interested in who they are; invite them to open up and share more. The majority of people are so involved in themselves they are unable to listen. Listening is a rare quality, and to meet a person who truly listens to you and absorbs your words is a gift.

4. Express Your Needs; Ask for What You Want

Often our emotions get activated from our 'needs' not being met. Don't expect your partner to guess what you want, or what you need, and when you need it. Each of us has more chance of getting what we need when we clearly ask for it. For many of us acknowledging our needs, even in simple matters, is a challenge because pride and ego can get in the way of us exposing our needs, weakness, insecurity or vulnerability. (See Marshall Rosenberg, *Nonviolent Communication*, in books section)

5. Talk About Yourself and not the Other Person

If you are talking about the other, ask yourself 'Is this my business, or is it their business?' The more you can stay with your own business, the easier it is to find happiness together. Avoid saying 'I feel that you...' or 'You always....' or 'You never...'

6. Express What You Feel

Do not be afraid about the other person rejecting you for sharing your deeper feelings, or for being honest and true. When feelings are expressed, in their purity, you communicate directly heart to heart, and 'touch' the other person. They will usually respond by opening up, not closing down. And you, yourself, will feel much lighter and expanded so expressing how or what you feel is a risk worth taking.

7. Communicate out of Present Moment

Talk about what you feel in your body, your heart and your soul and not about the thoughts passing through your mind. Most of us are usually absent from the present because we are 'busy thinking', which implies that we are rarely involved or rooted with our senses in *this* very moment. When we talk about the present, we naturally refer to the body, the heart and the soul because these are our bridges to the present, the place where we discover our authentic feelings and sensitivities.

8. Leave the Past in the Past

Avoid recycling your past stories or difficult situations. Once they are over they are over. Emotion is a tension that will cause you to keep dragging unhappiness into the present; be certain to express any withheld feelings related to any past incidents, so the charge/tension/unhappiness can leave your system. Avoid talking about your former lovers; it brings about comparison and jealousy that can easily spark off a bout of emotionality. Speak of a former lover only if you are being constructive by referring to an insight you have had about the past relationship or something you have learned about yourself through them.

9. Develop a Sense of Humor

Humor is the capacity to laugh at oneself, the ability to not take oneself too seriously. Humor demonstrates that a person is not very identified with *who* they are. Instead they can flip a statement around so that the laughter will be at their own expense. They are not laughing at other people, but with other people. The more distance you have to yourself, the greater your sense of humor will be. An emotional person generally lacks a sense of humor. They will be sensitive about the smallest things that are said and done; they will react to other people rather than respond. Lack of humor can sometimes be a symptom of emotion.

10. Do not Take Anything Personally

Each person is living in their own world, with their own issues. It is not to do with you. This is particularly important to remember when your partner gets emotional. Whatever hurtful things the person says to you they really do not mean so in their heart of hearts. Do your best not take the situation personally, even though it can be a challenge at times. Remember, emotional statements are poisonous so it is easy to become affected and emotional through the other person's emotionality. Stay rooted in your body, close your eyes, do not think about what they are saying, and allow the words to pass you by. Jump around to release any tension that may be arising in your own body.

11. One Person Cannot Fulfill All Your Expectations

The partner you have cannot be responsible for fulfilling all your needs and expectations. Other people in life may be able to support you as well. For instance if you like receiving massage and your partner does not like giving it, then go to a massage therapist instead of nagging and complaining about what you are not getting from them. Or if you enjoy to cook and your partner does not, don't get mad at them for not cooking for you once in while – go out to eat!

12. Never Tell Your Partner that They Are Emotional

Never tell your partner that they are emotional unless you have an agreement between you to help each other by lovingly pointing out emotions when they arise. As mentioned before, it is easier to recognize the emotions of your partner than your own. Even telling your partner that they are emotional can sometimes be indirectly emotional on your own part. Highly advisable is to remain out of your partner's business and bring the focus back to yourself.

13. Separate Home Life and Work Life

If you are working together during the day, do not drag your work home with you. Keep your personal time together free of business. If there is something important to talk about then make a specific appointment to discuss it. And when the meeting is over, quit talking about the issues or experiences. Talking about things distant from the present moment where you are together keeps you apart.

14. Avoid Talking Continuously about Your Children

Parents often talk endlessly to each other about their children, what they have done or said, with the result that the focus moves away from themselves as lovers, or as a couple. Very little time is taken for sharing or expressing being to being. Talk about yourselves instead of your children. Children benefit enormously from a loving relaxed environment at home, where they feel a cohesion between the parents, so it is healthy for the family life in general to keep yourselves in focus too, and not only the children.

15. Use Silence as Communication

Accustom yourselves to 'sharing silence' as a way of being together. Begin to notice the quality of silence, the depth of the silence, the sound of the silence, the music of the silence. Give a value to silence as a form communication between your being and inner world to the being and inner world of another. Often couples fill up gaps by talking about irrelevant matters, out of pure habit or because they find silence uncomfortable. Through constant chatter we easily can lose our connection to the present and love. When we talk all the time we lose contact with our feelings, because too much speaking actually prevents us from feeling our bodies.

16. Avoid Going to Sleep When You Are Emotional

If you have a fight it is best, if at all possible, to sort it out before you go to sleep. Unsolved problems/emotions can result in a night of restless sleep and you wake up in the morning unrefreshed and perhaps even more emotional and your day can easily be ruined.

17. Avoid Gossiping About Other People

Gossip can be a way of discharging emotion at a subtle level and should be avoided. Gossip is usually a bit poisonous and not very loving or supportive.

18. Use Touch to Communicate Your Feelings

Through touch we can communicate our love; hands are an extension of the heart. Do not rely on words alone to keep you in love. Spend time being together embracing in silence and awareness. An emotional person can often be 'difficult to touch', unduly sensitive and may complain that your touch is hurting them, whereas in reality your touch may be very gentle. Stored unexpressed feeling/emotion in the body is often experienced or perceived as pain in the body.

A person suffering depression or low-grade emotionality will benefit from regular massage. Touch connects a person to their body on a cellular level that can act as a bridge to the present moment and a sense of all being well.

19. When Emotional Avoid Making Love

When you are in intense emotion it is wiser *not* to make love. One of the by-products of emotion is that it can also produce sexual excitement, which will encourage you to finish sex with a conventional discharge through orgasm, thereby unconsciously creating more tension. When emotion causes excitement it is a big challenge to remain present and aware as suggested in tantric sex. Through emotional sex, as explained earlier, you can also easily deposit further tension in your system and inadvertently plant the seeds for the next fight. Make love when the wave of emotion has passed.

Chapter 13

PERSONAL EXPERIENCES

Eight Authentic Sharings After Learning the Difference between Emotion and Feeling

Many of the issues raised in the previous chapters are brought vividly to life through the sharing of personal experiences by couples who have attended our Making Love Seminars. Some of the sharings will contain references to sex because the contributors have been exploring tantric sex in tandem with a heightened awareness of their emotional states.

1. Sharing of experience from a couple:

Woman:

The conscious distinction between feeling and emotions was a great discovery for me. But the most important thing is, that I know that my partner and I have the same information. I feel his understanding and our awareness helps us in an acute situation to focus on the solution. I have learnt to express my feelings. Doing so, it was very helpful for me to know that unexpressed feelings become emotions. To know this was a motivation for me, since I do not want to accumulate more rubbish. And it is relaxing to know that my partner knows as well. For me, personally, I get a lot out of the physical body exertion after emotions have come up. I do a lot of exercise and during jogging I often reflect about the origin of my emotions. I have already found a lot of answers. The source of emotion lies mostly in childhood and some earlier phases of my life. These insights help me in dealing with myself but also in connection with other people. It is especially helpful in my partnership that we make love regularly. Then I feel more grounded and well and I can manage my whole life in a better way. And I am less emotional.

Man:

In the moment when something comes up, it is, at first, difficult to realize that I am probably emotional. Secondly, it is not easy to say, 'I am emotional'. But it is now possible for me to digest unexpressed feelings without hurting my partner. It is also important that I do not try to understand what is coming up, but that I just simply accept and release it. I feel strong in these moments for I am no more that much at the mercy of explosions and hurt.

2. Woman writing a few month after the seminar:

I wanted to share something with you about my emotions. In my relationship I face the problem that I close down as soon as I miss my partner's attention, believing that my partner does not really love me. And then I used to pretend I would not really need his attention, and that I can be as happy on my own. And I start to reject him, in order to punish him for not being nice enough to me.

Of course sometimes he feels hurt, but sometimes he is alert and stays with himself. These days I begin to realize how childish I have been in the past, and now it gets more and more easy to jump out of that emotional pattern.

3. Personal experience of woman during Making Love Retreat:

Here are two stories about my emotions. On the second day of the retreat we went to bed to make love. It was a bit difficult to come together and my partner told me about his fear of getting closer to me, his fear to open his heart to me. It hit me like a slap in the face and immediately I felt separated and rejected. I could not stay any longer in bed with him, so I took a walk in the forest, took a hot shower and returned to our room. I felt a bit better but still my heart felt closed, hurt and very sad.

During the evening meditation a few hours later all old pain came up and I recognized how my ex-husband used always to keep me at a distance in so many parts of our lives. One minute later I felt the distance between my father and me when I was a child, my longing for his love, for being close to him and the way he kept me at a distance. I discovered this to be the root of my emotional pattern. I was very angry, full of hate and I put this all in my dance. During the silence stage of the meditation, I felt all my sadness and cried my tears. After the meditation I was very tired but my body and my heart felt 'clean' and I felt my love and my connection with my boyfriend again.

Two days later during lunch we sat at the table, made a lot of jokes and I felt light and happy. He made a joke and said 'I think you should pay me for this making love course. How much money did 'X' (my ex- husband) get for 12 years?' In this moment I was able to tell my partner immediately, 'Oof, this hurts. Wow! It hurts very much.' And for one minute I started to cry, so I got up, went to the forest again and put all my anger and hate into the earth. I recognize that I had paid for love in many ways; I paid with money; I paid through 'betraying myself'; I paid through doing many things just to fulfill expectations of my parents, my ex-husband, my friends and my clients.

Behind this anger there was again a lot of pain, sadness and tears. And after crying a lot I returned to the seminar house, took a hot shower and met my partner in our room. We had a beautiful afternoon, enjoyed making love and I felt very peaceful, soft and gentle. Often when I get emotional my partner *does not* get emotional. And through the space this gives me it is possible for me to go deeper into the roots of my emotions. And it feels very healing and cleansing. But also there is fear to leave this 'emotional way of being' behind me. Who am I without these strong emotions? Do I still have my 'power' and 'independence' then? My heart knows that there is nothing to fear, but my ego is fighting like a lion.

4. Sharing by man, partner of woman above:

For me it is definitely easier to recognize emotions in my woman and sometimes (more and more) I can see how it affects me and inflames my emotions. The challenge is then (surprise, surprise) to not say to her 'you are emotional', but to stay and to feel my love for her. When I see emotions in her I say 'yeah that's difficult. But I cannot make you happy when you don't want to be happy'. Anyway, it is always a challenge. But now at least I don't want to *not* see her for several weeks as was common in the past. It is so much better since we got back from the seminar.

For myself I realized I am more the sort of always low-grade emotional type – 'don't touch me here and this feels not right and that's too hard' – a bit spiky and so on. On the other hand I *am* sensitive, so it is a walk on the line between being sensitive and being prickly. I used to 'discharge' while driving a car. I would shout at other drivers and blink with the lights and be a raging bull. And I would feel so right because they really drive terribly! After the workshop I remembered that my father would be the same way; he was as gentle as a lamb until he entered a car and got on the road; he'd become an irate avenger! So today, seeing this, I can now drive in a relaxed manner – mostly. Sometimes it comes like a rush through my veins and there I go – yelling and blinking for eight seconds, then I see myself and laugh.

5. Report of a woman, some years after participating with her husband in one of our seminars:

For years I have been working in training's and courses on my emotions in every day life. The emotions never leave me alone. They are always there and they are challenging me. My emotions have confused and overcharged me over a long period of time. They determine my life to a high degree and they influenced my relationships in a way that it was barely possible to relax lovingly into very close relating. Very often I simply felt at the mercy of my emotions. That happens quite often to me, but with your new way of separating emotions and feelings, of sorting them out and dealing with them, I received a very helpful tool. I could quite soon recognize physical sensations and thoughts quite clearly and deal with them accordingly. But the emotions were still confusing and burdening.

Still today I sometimes do not really know why I react in a certain way. When and why do I feel good today? What influences me? For me it was a big clarification and a relief to hear about the distinction between feelings and emotions. As soon as I realize that I do not feel free enough anymore to turn to the person with me with an open heart; when a sort of channel, a tightness, is building around me; when I withdraw and feel powerless, or when I fight for something, I know that I am emotional. It helps to know then that a great part of my reaction is connected to something old, something past, that is stored in me, which has little to do with the here and now.

It is relieving for me, and also for the other, when I am invaded by emotions and I know thereby that these have nothing to do with the present situation or the person I am with. It eases me a lot to say 'I am furious, sad, disappointed and this has nothing to do with you'. Living together with my husband I experience this situation often. By saying 'I am emotional', at least a part of the tension dissolves.

In the sexual encounters with my husband I am often emotional. Something about my day keeps me busy; I am not good at letting go or, due to some incident, I am confronted with emotional resistance, and therefore I cannot engage physically or on the level of feelings. If I have to say then 'I am emotional', this relaxes us both, and more is not needed. He knows then, that it has nothing to do with him. Often we start talking about what keeps me occupied, and I can articulate my needs and thereby I often let go of the tensions.

When the other is emotional, it is difficult as a partner not to get pulled into one's own emotions, so that both are finally reacting from the base of their hurt feelings. We practice to let the other be with his/her momentary experience; not to help; not to persuade; not to feel responsible and not to 'do' anything for the other. By staying connected to myself I, therefore, do not react emotionally, and I can still support the other in his emotions. I remain connected with my partner. I experience that if there are strong emotions, especially rage but also grief and pain, it is important to give myself permission to withdraw from the other person in order become quiet and clear. I have to consciously make the decision to do that, knowing that it is better for me and us. This is often difficult for me, and I experience it as an act of will. I have rather the tendency to cling in such a situation than to let go.

Once I had repressed my emotions so strongly that I lost control with all my helplessness, rage and pain and crashed a toilet seat. I did not manage any longer to channel and release my very strong emotions into a non-dangerous physical activity. The power and might of my emotions, as well as the loss of control, shocked me a lot. After this incident I got more aware. I took the emotions more seriously. And I can now comprehend how violence can happen in relationships. After that we hung up a punching bag, which can help everybody in the family to express emotions that are stuck.

If one of us is strongly emotional, a sexual encounter is a taboo for me. As I am naturally receptive as a woman, I feel reluctant to add to the tensions in my body because usually we go into hot sex. In the meantime we have sensitized ourselves so that we do not burden each other anymore with unnecessary emotions. I am often not aware of my own reactions to the unexpressed emotions of my husband; it is my body that reacts and resists the flow, or my heart does not open during the encounter of lovemaking. I could also say, for some reason, I could simply not relax and surrender, though I do not feel emotional myself. Also in these situations we talk with each other. This is very important. I have the impression that due to the distinction between feelings and emotions we can be much more free with each other. And we enjoy ourselves when we experience that we are disconnected from old stories and totally connected with our feeling in the here and now. Through this we attain a state of enormous presence.

6. Experiences of woman who participated in our seminars several times:

Two years ago, I learnt in your seminar about the distinction between emotions and feelings. It appealed to me and ever since we try to apply it to our everyday life. First of all we pinned the 'detection list' on how to recognize emotions on our fridge. This is the place in our home, which is frequented often at all times of the day. This permanent (often unpleasant) reminder was a great support, especially in the beginning. Very quickly we reduced our daily arguments as a couple to the minimum. We had not been aware of many of our quarrels as they had already belonged to our daily routine. Sentences beginning with 'you always…/you never…' were a part of the introduction in our fights. As soon as one of us uses these sentences today, we mostly recognize our emotional state on our own, and most of the time we know what to do. Quickly I found out that I used to take everything very personally. In the course of the year I became more aware of many of my behavior patterns. Some of them I could stop immediately. And if I do not succeed sometimes, I can now, more easily and most importantly quickly, withdraw from the situation.

Previously, I was definitely aware of it when I was in one of my emotional states, but I didn't have the necessary tools to free myself from it. Often by trying to explain (by talking, talking, talking), everything got worse and took much more time. Now many daily stressful situations with the partner and primarily with the children have 'simply' dissolved.

I can remember a situation on the phone with a very grumpy relative. During this brief conversation he started to unload his emotions unconsciously. Instead of listening to him with patience, I waited till he took the first breath of air and interrupted him, in a very friendly but decisively way, by saying that I had to leave for a date. Immediately, he also interrupted himself, and we said goodbye. Previously, I had felt rather exposed in such situations, and I felt obliged to listen and to try to 'help'.

Now being able to draw a distinction between feelings and emotions, I do not have the impression anymore that I am hurting the other if I do not, out of my old habit, engage with him. I feel less burdened, for I do not let myself be used as a dump of the emotional tensions of others any more. With this daily exercise in my social environment it gets ever clearer, how often I have dumped and released emotions, such as anger, huffiness, complaint and also total euphoria. Often I see myself in others and try to act differently (and not to react) – ever more often with success!

Once my partner was in a depression for days without my being affected very much or without me pulling myself down. I was in a good mood. My 'very well meant' advice to him to move his body was followed, but unfortunately without success. 'No matter how much I vacuum, clean or drink water nothing helps,' my partner insinuated in a harsh tone. As soon as he had said that, I felt a pressure on my head and my previous compassion was gone. Fortunately, I did not react with a counterattack; rather, I had the insight to abstain from further advice, as a kind of defense. Shortly after our 'states' had dissolved, we had to laugh so much about the humor of the situation.

The ongoing awareness of my emotional situation has become a part of my daily thinking, feeling and acting. Thereby I have received the impression that even more subtle levels are opening up, and that it is therefore ever more dodgy to recognize the present emotional states. It is quite easy for me to identify emotions that derive from old hurt or memories. Most difficulties are created by my mind that gets ever more tricky and produces emotions without any external trigger and without me realizing it. Altogether in the past two years much more relaxation and serenity has become manifest inside of me. I found more under-standing for myself. I am very grateful for that. The life with my partner and the children has become more loving, intimate, simple and above all more humorous. We can laugh about the permanent shifts of our internal states, and we joke about the many, many 'traps' in which we get caught again and again.

7. Sharing of personal experience by woman returning to our seminar:

As I listened to the lecture on emotions and feelings for the very first time, I believed that I am not a very emotional person, since it is very rare that I fight with my husband. Hearing the lecture now, one year later, for the second time, I discovered and had to admit to myself that I am indeed very emotional, in a subliminal, but therefore almost continuous, manner especially toward my husband. I got aware of that, as I understood the concept of 'subliminal or low grade emotionality'. Since I was raised in a very controlled manner (my parents and other adults gave me credit for being so 'balanced'), I always tried to avoid conflicts with my partner. As soon as I felt hurt or I anticipated a conflict, I withdrew immediately, which felt like an internal freezing. Always when an emotion was touched inside of me, I repressed it immediately, instead of expressing it in the form of an argument or as an accusation. I sort of 'recycled' it. Over the years these recycled emotions built an almost unbreakable wall between us, which finally impeded any loving feeling. Ever since I have opened more towards my partner, I realize that I am quickly highly emotional, for it is the first time for me to perceive and allow my emotions. This triggers a lot of fear in me. At the same time it can be really rewarding if I succeed to see that it is 'merely' an emotion. What a relief!

8. Sharing from a man after attending a seminar:

I was much impressed by your sound ideas and reflections about the difference between emotions and feelings. In addition to the relevance of this concept to couples, I am sure it has a great impact on peace building (e.g. in ethnical conflicts like in former Yugoslavia). I am working on this subject, comparing several concepts of peace building like *Communication without Violence* (by Marshall Rosenberg), mediation, systemic solutions (based on systemic family therapy and systemic coaching), and system constellation approaches (based on the family constellation approaches of Bert Hellinger). All these 'methods' are helpful; they all stress very much the importance of dealing with the emotions/feelings of the conflict parties to reach a long-lasting solution of the conflict, but none of them sees the difference between feelings and emotions (just as I did not see it until you told us!) For example, the conflict in former Yugoslavia gets its energy partly from the lost fight of the Serbians with the Muslims 600 years ago on the 'Amselfeld'. It is still in the mind of the Serbians, that they lost it. I think everything related to this is more an emotion than a feeling. And on the other hand, every day there are new wounds, which give rise to feelings. If nobody sees the difference, the energies of emotions and feelings will always mix in a crazy way, and the conflict cannot be solved (better to say: we will never reach closer to a conflict solution). For me, these aspects of feelings and emotions are very interesting for peace building concepts. Maybe this aspect fits to your book as an additional application.

Not relating to your work on emotions, but definitely relating to feelings, I'd like to share a picture that came into my mind the last days: Conventional sex is like mountain climbing, straight up to peak. Tantric sex, as I learned it from many other 'neo tantra' teachers, is still like climbing mountains, reaching much more higher peaks than in conventional sex and dancing a while near the peak, until you reach it. Tantric sex, as I learned it with you, happens also in the beautiful mountain landscape. But long before you start getting exhausted of climbing the peak, you find that there are lovely meadows, marvelous forests, small brooks with clear water you can drink. So you just start walking round the mountain. From time to time you can see the peak; you can climb up to it whenever you want, but usually there is no need to do, because it is so beautiful right where you are.

Appendix: Inspiration in Love

Short excerpts from Osho's talks have been incorporated into the text. Here they can be read in full.

Question by Tallis: *'Beloved Osho, what is love?'*
Love is the radiance, the fragrance of knowing oneself, of being oneself. Tallis is very young – he is only nine – but he is far ahead of his age. His mental age must be almost double that, near about eighteen, hence the question.

Love is overflowing joy. Love is when you have seen who you are; then there is nothing left except to share your being with others. Love is when you have seen that you are not separate from existence. Love is when you have felt an organic, orgasmic unity with all that is. Love is not a relationship, Tallis. Love is a state of being; it has nothing to do with anybody else. One is not in love, one is love. And of course when one is love, one is in love – but that is an outcome, a by-product, that is not the source. The source is that one is love. And who can be love?

Certainly, if you are not aware of who you are, you cannot be love. You will be fear. Fear is just the opposite of love. Remember, hate is not the opposite of love, as people think; hate is love standing upside down, it is not the opposite of love. The real opposite of love is fear. In love one expands, in fear one shrinks. In fear one becomes closed, in love one opens. In fear one doubts, in love one trusts. In fear one is left lonely, in love one disappears; hence there is no question of loneliness at all. When one is not, how can one be lonely? Then these trees and the birds and the clouds and the sun and the stars are still within you. Love is when you have known your inner sky.

And Tallis, this is the right moment, the right age, to enter into the world of love. This is the time when parents, the society, the state and the church go on poisoning children and making them afraid. This is the time when fear is created by the exploiters. This is the time when society reduces small children to slaves; and one can be reduced to a slave only if great fear is created. This is the time also – if the society is sane and is not dominated by stupid politicians and priests, if the society is not pathological – when the society will help the children to become more and more loving, will help the children to know more about beauty, about music, about poetry, about dance, about meditation. This is the time when the child can simply take a plunge without any difficulties.

Later on it will become more and more difficult, because as you grow old, fears also grow older and stronger. As you grow old the ego becomes more strengthened. As you grow old your capacity to learn decreases. As you grow old you become more and more cowardly, afraid of the unknown. The young child is free of fear; children are born without any fear. If the society can help and support them to remain without fear, can help them to climb the trees and the mountains, and swim the oceans and the rivers, if the society can help them in every possible way to become adventurers, adventurers of the unknown, and if the society can create a great enquiry instead of giving them dead beliefs, then the children will turn into great lovers, lovers of life – and that is true religion. There is no higher religion than love.

Osho, transcribed teachings, The Guest chapter 6

Love has to be moved from category of emotions

Question: *So often a feeling that I can't describe fills my heart and my whole being. During the other morning's discourse it felt like overwhelming love for you and the whole. But now I realize that the same feeling or a very, very similar feeling also comes up in fear, anguish, throbbing pain, helplessness and frustration. I am trembling and confused. Can you say something?*

There is certainly something very similar in very different

emotions: the 'overwhelmingness'. It may be love, it may be hate, it may be anger – it can be anything. If it is too much then it gives you a sense of being overwhelmed by something. Even pain and suffering can create the same experience, but 'overwhelmingness' has no value in itself. It simply shows you are an emotional being. This is typically the indication of an emotional personality. When it is anger, it is all anger. And when it is love, it is all love. It almost becomes drunk with the emotion, blind. And whatever action comes out of it is wrong. Even if it is overwhelming love, the action that will come out of it is not going to be right. Reduced to its base, whenever you are overwhelmed by any emotion you lose all reason, you lose all sensitivity, you lose your heart in it. It becomes almost like a dark cloud in which you are lost. Then whatever you do is going to be wrong.

Love is not to be a part of your emotions. Ordinarily that's what people think and experience, but anything overwhelming is very unstable. It comes like a wind and passes by, leaving you behind, empty, shattered, in sadness and in sorrow.

According to those who know man's whole being – his mind, his heart and his being – love has to be an expression of your being, not an emotion. Emotion is very fragile, very changing. One moment it seems that is all. Another moment you are simply empty. So the first thing to do is to take love out of this crowd of overwhelming emotions.

Love is not overwhelming. On the contrary, love is a tremendous insight, clarity, sensitivity, awareness. But that kind of love rarely exists, because very few people ever reach to their being.

Osho, transcribed teachings, Om Shantih, Shantih, Shantih, 17

Fear is the absence of love

Question: *You say fear is the opposite of love. Have you any practical or impractical suggestions how one can drop fear?*

Love is existential; fear is only the absence of love. And the problem with any absence is that you cannot do anything directly about it. Fear is like darkness. What can you do about darkness directly? You cannot drop it, you cannot throw it out, you cannot bring it in. There is no way to relate with darkness without bringing light in. The way to darkness goes via light. If you want darkness, put the light off; if you don't want darkness, put the light on. But you will have to do something with light, not with darkness at all.

The same is true about love and fear: love is light, fear is darkness. The person who becomes obsessed with fear will never be able to resolve the problem. It is like wrestling with darkness – you are bound to be exhausted sooner or later, tired and defeated. And the miracle is, defeated by something which is not there at all! And when one is defeated, one certainly feels how powerful the darkness is, how powerful the fear is, how powerful the ignorance is, how powerful the unconscious is. And they are not powerful at all – they don't exist in the first place.

Never fight with the non existential. That's where all the ancient religions got lost. Once you start fighting with the non existential you are doomed. Your small river of consciousness will be lost in the non existential desert – and it is infinite.

Hence, the first thing to remember is: don't make a problem out of fear. Love is the question. Something can be done about love immediately; there is no need to wait or postpone. Start loving! And it is a natural gift from God to you, or from the whole, whichever term you like. If you are brought up in a religious way, then God; if you are not brought up in a religious way, then the whole, the universe, the existence.

Remember, love is born with you; it is your intrinsic quality. All that is needed is to give it way – to make a passage for it, to let it flow, to allow it to happen. We are all blocking it, holding it back. We are so miserly about love, for the simple reason that we have been taught a certain economics. That economics is perfectly right about the outside world: if you have so much money and you go on giving that money to people, soon you will be a beggar, soon you will have to beg yourself. By giving money you will lose it.

This economics, this arithmetic has entered into our blood, bones and marrow. It is true about the outside world – nothing is wrong in it – but it is not true about the inner journey. There, a totally different arithmetic functions: the more you give, the more you have; the less you give, the less you have. If you don't give at all you will lose your natural qualities. They will become stagnant, closed; they will go underground. Finding no expression they will shrink and die.

Osho, transcribed teachings, Come, Come, yet again come, 10

Books and Recommended Reading

Osho, book references and source supplied with each quotation.

Long, Barry. *Raising Children in Love, Justice and Truth*. Barry Long Books, 1998

Long, Barry. *Making Love – Sexual Love the Divine Way*. Barry Long Books, CD Audio.

Long, Barry. *Love Brings All to Life*, Barry Long Books, CD Audio

Richardson, Diana. *The Heart of Tantric Sex*. O Books, 2002 (First edition as *The Love Keys – The Art of Ecstatic Sex*, 1999)

Richardson, Diana. *Tantric Orgasm for Women*. Destiny Books, 2004

Richardson, Diana & Michael. *Tantric Sex for Men*. Destiny Books, 2010

Rosenberg, Marshall. *Nonviolent Communication: A language of life*. Puddle Dancer, 2003

Ruiz, Don Miguel. *The Four Agreements*. Amber-Allen, 1997

Ruiz, Don Miguel. *Mastery of Love*. Amber-Allen, 1999

Tolle, Eckhart. *The Power of Now* and *A New Earth: Awakening to your Life's purpose*. Penguin Books, 2006

BOOKS

O is a symbol of the world, of oneness and unity. In different cultures it also means the "eye," symbolizing knowledge and insight. We aim to publish books that are accessible, constructive and that challenge accepted opinion, both that of academia and the "moral majority."

Our books are available in all good English language bookstores worldwide. If you don't see the book on the shelves ask the bookstore to order it for you, quoting the ISBN number and title. Alternatively you can order online (all major online retail sites carry our titles) or contact the distributor in the relevant country, listed on the copyright page.

See our website **www.o-books.net** for a full list of over 500 titles, growing by 100 a year.

And tune in to myspiritradio.com for our book review radio show, hosted by June-Elleni Laine, where you can listen to the authors discussing their books.

mySpiritRadio